Perfect Patchwork Bags

15 Projects to Sew

From Clutches to Market Bags

Sue Kim
with Veronica Yang

stashBOOKS.
an imprint of C&T Publishing

Text and artwork copyright © 2016 by Sue Kim and Veronica Yang

Photography and artwork copyright © 2016 by C&T Publishing, Inc.

Publisher: Amy Marson

Creative Director: Gailen Runge

Editor: Liz Aneloski

Technical Editors: Julie Waldman and Amanda Siegfried

Cover/Book Designer: April Mostek

Production Coordinator: Zinnia Heinzmann

Production Editors: Alice Mace Nakanishi and Jennifer Warren

Illustrator: Aliza Shalit

Photo Assistant: Sarah Frost

How-to photography by Sue Kim, style photography by Page + Pixel, and instructional photography by Diane Pedersen, unless otherwise noted

Published by Stash Books, an imprint of C&T Publishing, Inc., P.O. Box 1456, Lafayette, CA 94549

Library of Congress Cataloging-in-Publication Data

Names: Kim, Sue, 1969- author. | Yang, Veronica, author.

Title: Perfect patchwork bags : 15 projects to sew - from clutches to market bags / Sue Kim with Veronica Yang.

Description: Lafayette, CA : C&T Publishing, Inc., [2016]

Identifiers: LCCN 2015043745 | ISBN 9781617451454 (soft cover)

Subjects: LCSH: Handbags. | Patchwork--Patterns.

Classification: LCC TT667 .K524 2016 | DDC 746.46--dc23

LC record available at http://lccn.loc.gov/2015043745

Printed in China

10 9 8 7 6 5 4 3 2 1

Acknowledgments

My daughter, Veronica, first started hand sewing from an early age. Unfortunately her first piece did not turn out the greatest. She didn't quite know where she had gone wrong on her first pair of pants.

But thankfully, that didn't discourage her from the sewing world that I was so engrossed in. In fact, it made her want to do better, and later it even inspired her to become a designer— just like me! After a long journey, she started writing this book with me as a joint author. Three of the patterns included in this book were made by my daughter. In addition, she helped me with the fabric choices, color matching, and making of the samples on all the other patterns that are included in the book!

Through this experience it made me realize just how much my little girl had grown up!

So, I would like to take this time to give a special thanks to my daughter, who was there through the whole process. Also, I would like to thank my husband, Jung, and my two sons, Chan and Caleb, who are always there to support me. My thanks also go out to June; Hye Kyung, Jung; John; and Christine for helping me draw the patterns and making the samples with me.

Introduction

Quilting is one of those things you just can't stop once you start. I think anyone who's ever quilted will agree wholeheartedly. When I'm sewing block after block of patchwork pieces, I'm always curious to see the result of adding the next color … and the time flies by.

Quilting is for more than large blankets. Don't be intimidated by the many pieces of fabric. If you can sew a straight line, you can quilt. If you're not a quilter, this book will introduce you to the joy of sewing together piece after piece of fabric. If you are a quilter, you already understand how fun and rewarding it is.

I hope to introduce not only the enjoyment of quilting, but the practicality as well! I can almost guarantee that every sewist in the world has a stash of leftover fabrics. I realized that my leftover scraps were just enough to make a bag, clutch, or purse. The projects start with smaller bags and clutches, a great place to begin.

My other inspiration for writing this book was to introduce new, sleek bag designs that fit well with our modern world. Hopefully, these bags will be able to pique an interest in the younger generations for this traditional craft!

Aimed toward new quilters, this book includes projects that can be made with a regular sewing machine and without the need for any special feet. The quilting itself is also made simple by using fusible interfacing.

So, let's throw away the stereotype that quilting is a *special* genre for *special* people and let's start on your quilting journey today!

Contents

Sewing and Quilting Information

Applying a Magnetic Snap

Attach the magnetic snap onto the fabric, following the manufacturer's instructions. Most of the snaps attach according to the following steps:

1. Cut a small piece of fusible interfacing at least ¼″ larger than the snap on all sides. Apply the interfacing to the wrong side of the fabric, centered on the snap location. Center the snap disk on the interfacing.

2. Use a pencil to mark the interfacing where it will need to be cut for the prongs. **FIGURE A**

3. Carefully snip the little holes for the prongs. **FIGURE B**

4. Insert the prongs of one side of the magnetic snap through the right side of the fabric. **FIGURE C**

5. Push the prongs through the holes toward the wrong side of the fabric and through the interfacing.

6. Place the disk over the prongs. Fold the prongs outward. Finish by attaching the other half of the magnetic snap to the other piece of fabric in the same manner. **FIGURE D**

A

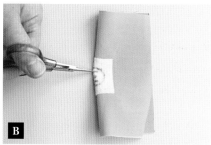

B

C

D

Clipping and Trimming the Seam

Clipping

Make small V-shaped cuts on the inner (concave seams) or outer (convex seams) curves to help them lie flat when turned to the right side. Always clip within the seam allowance, not beyond it. **FIGURE E**

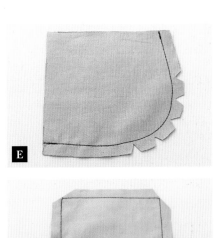

Trimming

With the piece wrong side out, trim off the excess fabric at the corners to reduce the bulk and create a sharp corner when you turn the piece right side out. **FIGURE F**

Connecting an Adjustable Buckle

1. Thread a strap over the middle bar of a slider strap adjuster. Fold ½″ from the end of the strap. **FIGURE G**

2. Fold the strap over the middle bar about 2″ and pin it onto the strap. Sew the strap together using a box shape, as shown. **FIGURE H**

3. Insert the other end of the strap into a lobster clip. **FIGURE I**

4. Lay the slider strap adjuster right side up and thread the end of the long strap through the buckle. **FIGURE J**

5. Insert the loose end of the strap into the other lobster clip. Fold ½″ from the end of the strap. **FIGURE K**

6. Fold the strap over the lobster clip and pin it onto the strap. Sew the strap together using a box shape. **FIGURE L**

7. Adjust the strap to your desired length. **FIGURE M**

Sewing Pockets

Use the methods below to make the pockets for the projects.

Standard Pocket

1. Cut 2 pocket pieces following the instructions in your pattern.

2. Sew the pocket with right sides together, leaving 2½˝ open on one side for turning. Trim the corner seams (see Trimming, page 7). **FIGURE N**

3. Turn the pocket right side out and use a sharp tool to push the corners out. Fold the seam allowances of the opening to the inside and press. Pin the opening and topstitch along the top, ⅛˝ from the edge, backstitching at both ends. **FIGURE O**

4. Place the pocket on the right side of the lining, with the topstitched edge facing upward. Topstitch the pocket in place on 3 sides, starting at the top of one side, sewing across the bottom and back up to the top, and backstitching at both ends. You can stitch one or more divider lines if you wish. **FIGURE P**

Elastic Pocket

If an elastic pocket sits at the base of your bag, use the bottom edge of the lining pattern as the pattern for the sides and corners of the pocket. Add 1½″–2½″ width to the center of the pocket piece to allow for gathers. Determine the desired height of the pocket and add 1¼″ at the top for the double fold to encase the elastic band. Cut out the pocket.

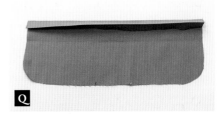

1. To create the casing for the elastic, double fold the top edge of the fabric piece. **FIGURE Q**

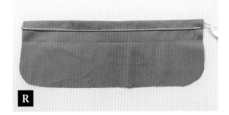

2. Pin and sew along the bottom edge of the fold line, backstitching at both ends.

3. Attach a safety pin to one end of the elastic.

4. Insert the safety pin into one open end of the casing. **FIGURE R**

5. Work the safety pin through the length of the casing, stopping to stitch the unpinned end of the elastic within the seamline at the entry edge. Continue to work the safety pin through the casing. Pull it out the open end, adjust the gathers, and pin the second (exit) end to secure the elastic temporarily. **FIGURE S**

6. To make the bottom gathers, sew a line of hand or machine basting stitches on the fabric, within the seam allowance along the bottom edge of the pocket piece. Leave a few inches of thread at each end. **FIGURE T**

7. Place the pocket piece on the back lining piece. The right side of the lining piece will meet the wrong side of the pocket. Pin along the bottom edge, making sure to pin at each end. Pull one end of the basting stitch thread and then the other end of the basting thread to match the bottom of the back lining piece. Pin and sew the 2 pieces together, adjusting the elastic to match the lining. Backstitch on both ends and cut the excess elastic. Sew the pocket divider lines at the desired intervals. **FIGURE U**

Zipper Pocket

1. To make the pocket, draw the zipper rectangle onto the wrong side of one zipper pocket piece. The rectangle will be ⅜″ tall and the length will be 1″ shorter than your zipper length. Place the zipper pocket piece and the lining piece with right sides together. Pin in place and sew all the way around the zipper pocket line.
FIGURE A

2. Cut down the center and to each corner, as indicated on the zipper pocket pattern, cutting through both layers of fabric.
FIGURE B

3. Fold the pocket fabric through the opening toward the wrong side of the lining.
FIGURE C

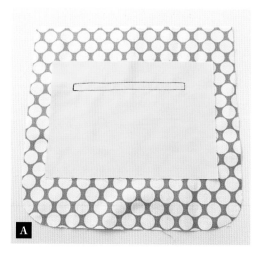

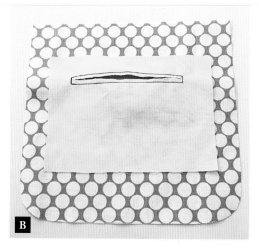

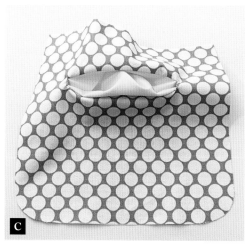

4. Press. The right side of the lining will look as shown.
FIGURE E

5. Place the zipper onto the wrong side of the lining unit. Match the right side of the zipper with the wrong side of the lining unit. Pin and stitch the zipper in place close to the folded edge of the fabric, backstitching at both ends.
FIGURE F

6. Place the other zipper pocket piece right sides together with the first piece. Without stitching the bag lining, stitch the 2 pocket pieces together all around, ⅜˝ from the edge.
FIGURE G

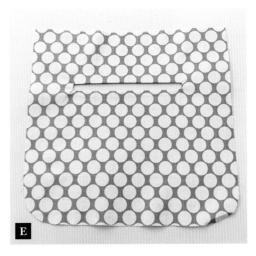

E

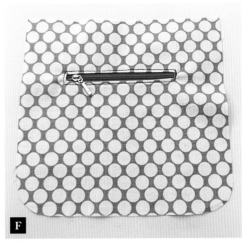

F

G

Adding Piping

1. Leaving the first 1˝–2˝ of your piping unstitched, stitch the piping onto your fabric, aligning the long raw edges. Use a zipper foot on your machine, if you have one, to help you stitch closer to the piping.

2. Stop stitching when you are 3˝–4˝ from the end of the piping and backstitch.

3. Trim off excess piping, leaving about 1˝ of overlap with the beginning end of the piping.

4. Remove a few of the original piping stitches at the second end of the piping and trim off about ½˝ of the inner core of the piping.

5. Fold the short raw edge in ¼˝ to the inside of the piping and finger-press the fold. **FIGURE A**

6. Place the first end of the piping into the folded second end. Pin and sew to finish. **FIGURE B**

Installing an Eyelet

1. Mark the position of the eyelet by tracing the *inside* of the eyelet; punch or cut out the hole. **FIGURE C**

2. Place the eyelet onto the anvil with the barrel pointing up.

3. Insert the eyelet barrel into the hole from the right side of the fabric through to the wrong side. **FIGURE D**

4. Place the eyelet washer on top of the barrel with the teeth pointing down. **FIGURE E**

5. Place the setter tool on top of the eyelet with the stud end in the eyelet barrel and hit the setter using a hammer. Do this until the eyelet opens up and clings firmly onto the fabric. **FIGURES F & G**

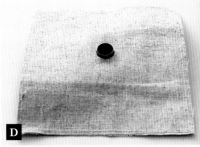

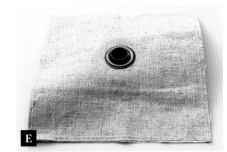

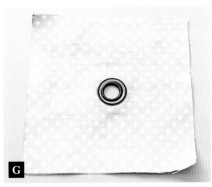

Back side of finished eyelet

Making a Strap

Strap A

1. Fold the strap in half lengthwise, wrong sides together, and press to make a crease. Open the strap with the wrong side facing you. Fold each long side of the strap in toward the center and press. **FIGURE A**

A

2. Fold in half again along the center crease and press. Topstitch ⅛″ from each long edge. **FIGURE B**

B

Strap B

1. Fold one short end of the strap in ½″ and press. **FIGURE C**

2. Follow Strap A, Step 1 (above), to fold the strap.

3. Topstitch down one long side, across the folded edge, and up the other long side to finish.

C

Strap C

1. Fold both short ends of the strap in ½″ and press.

2. Follow Strap A, Step 1 to fold the strap.

3. Topstitch around all 4 sides of the strap to finish.

Choosing Fabrics

I love to use my fabric scraps, but if you don't have enough, fat eighth bundles (available at your local quilting and fabric stores or online) are a great way to get small amounts of a variety of quilting-weight cotton and linen/cotton fabrics that go well together.

Linen/cotton is a little heavier than quilting-weight cotton, so when choosing your fabrics, you will need to decide the feel you want for your finished bag.

Sewing and Pressing

When sewing and piecing, be sure to use the seam allowance noted in the project instructions. When piecing, you can press your seam allowances either open or to one side, unless a specific direction is noted in the instructions.

Tools and Supplies

Piecing

Even if you have never tried quilting before, you will not have to gather too many materials. However, having a rotary cutter, cutting mat, and ruler will help you measure and cut the pieces much more easily and accurately.

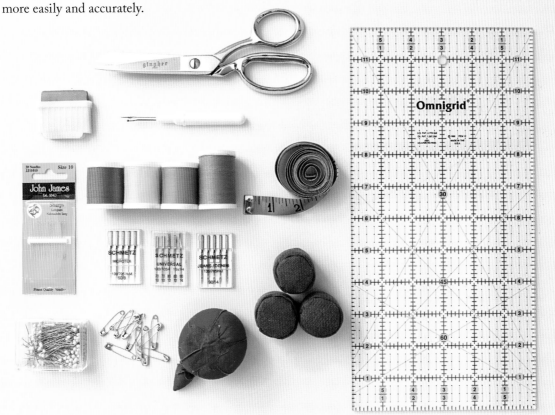

ROTARY CUTTER

Using a rotary cutter takes a little practice, but after a few minutes you'll understand what a great tool this is. Apply an even amount of pressure, cut away from yourself, and be sure to keep your fingers out of the way. This cutter is sharp! Be sure to close the cutter after every cut and store it out of children's reach.

Rotary cutter

ROTARY CUTTING MAT

You must use a mat specially made for cutting with a rotary cutter. These mats are self-healing (the slices go away) and they don't ruin your rotary cutter blade.

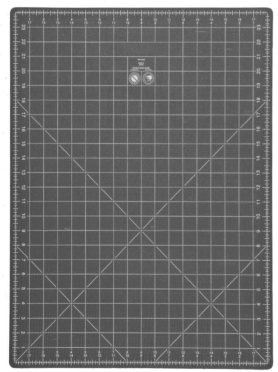

Cutting mat

RULER

You must also use an acrylic ruler specially made for cutting with a rotary cutter. These have markings to help you cut accurately and will not ruin your cutting blades. They come in various sizes and brands. I recommend that you use 6″ × 12″ and 6½″ × 6½″ rulers.

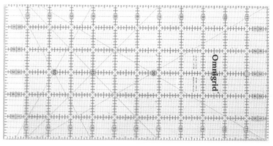

Ruler

Quilting

Quilting the pieced sections is optional.

The projects featured in this book do not require a special foot on the sewing machine for the piecing or the quilting. Adding fusible interfacing on the back of the pieced sections makes the piecing stable and easy to quilt. You can quilt next to the seamline (in-the-ditch) if you press the seams of your piecing to one side. This method is very beginner-friendly, thanks to the seamline you can follow!

Tablet Sleeve and Cell Phone Sleeve

FINISHED SIZES: Tablet Sleeve: 10" wide × 7¾" high • Phone Sleeve: 7" wide × 4⅜" high

These sleeves are perfect for cell phones and tablets! They have hook-and-loop tape closures, allowing users easy access to their devices. What's more, this pattern is easy to make and can be completed by sewists of all skill levels! The quilting in this pattern does not need much prior experience, making it accessible to anyone. With its unique zigzag flap patchwork and practical design, this sleeve makes a great gift!

note

You can omit the dark- and light-colored fabrics for the flap patchwork and make your tablet flap from a single fabric. Enough fabric is included.

MATERIALS for Tablet Sleeve

6 different dark-colored fabrics and 6 different light-colored fabrics for flap exterior patchwork (See the cutting list on the next page for sizes.)

⅜ yard of 44″-wide heavyweight home decorator or quilting-weight cotton for one-fabric exterior (and flap, if you wish)

⅜ yard for lining

1 yard of 20″-wide lightweight fusible interfacing

5″ of 1″-wide hook-and-loop tape (nonfusible)

1 yard of piping

MATERIALS for Cell Phone Sleeve

4 different dark-colored fabrics and 4 different light-colored fabrics for flap exterior patchwork (See the cutting list on the next page for sizes.)

¼ yard of 44″-wide heavyweight home decorator or quilting-weight cotton for one-fabric exterior (and flap, if you wish)

¼ yard for lining

⅜ yards of 20″-wide lightweight fusible interfacing

5″ of 1″-wide hook-and-loop tape (nonfusible)

⅝ yard of piping

note

• *A ¼″ seam allowance is included for the patchwork.*

• *A ⅜″ seam allowance is included on the patterns.*

• *Backstitch at the beginning and end of each seam.*

Flap Patchwork

CUTTING for Tablet Sleeve Flap Patchwork

Dark-colored fabrics

From the 6 fabrics:

- Cut 1 piece 1″ × 28″.

- Cut 2 pieces 1″ × 21″.

- Cut 2 pieces 1″ × 12″.

- Cut 1 piece 1″ × 5″.

Light-colored fabrics

From the 6 fabrics:

- Cut 1 piece 1¾″ × 28″.

- Cut 2 pieces 1¾″ × 21″.

- Cut 2 pieces 1¾″ × 12″.

- Cut 1 piece 1¾″ × 5″.

CUTTING for Cell Phone Sleeve Flap Patchwork

Dark-colored fabrics

From the 4 fabrics:

- Cut 1 piece 1″ × 18″.

- Cut 1 piece 1″ × 16″.

- Cut 1 piece 1″ × 12″.

- Cut 1 piece 1″ × 7″.

Light-colored fabrics

From the 4 fabrics:

- Cut 1 piece 1¾″ × 18″.

- Cut 1 piece 1¾″ × 16″.

- Cut 1 piece 1¾″ × 12″.

- Cut 1 piece 1¾″ × 7″.

Patchwork

1. Arrange the light-colored fabric strips and dark-colored fabric strips in pairs of the same length.

2. With right sides together, sew the 1″ strip and 1¾″ strip together. Press the strip set open. **FIGURE A**

3. Repeat Steps 1 and 2 to sew all the pairs of strips (strip sets) together.

4. Using a rotary cutter, cut the strip sets into 2¼″ × 2¼″ squares. **FIGURE B**

A   B

5. Arrange the squares into rows (42 blocks into 6 rows of 7 squares each for the tablet sleeve, and 20 blocks into 4 rows of 5 squares each for the cell phone sleeve).

6. Sew the blocks into rows and press.

7. Sew the rows together and press. **FIGURE C**

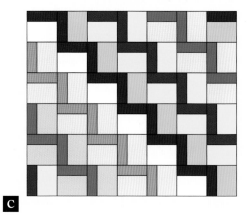

C

8. Using the Tablet Sleeve Flap pattern or the Cell Phone Sleeve Flap pattern, cut a piece of interfacing and fuse it onto the wrong side of the flap exterior piece, following the manufacturer's instructions. Quilt by hand or machine. **FIGURE D**

Sleeve Construction

Using either the Tablet Sleeve Flap and Tablet Front and Back patterns (pullout page P2) **OR** the Cell Phone Sleeve Flap and Cell Phone Sleeve Front and Back patterns (pullout page P1), cut out the following pieces and transfer all points and references to the fabric.

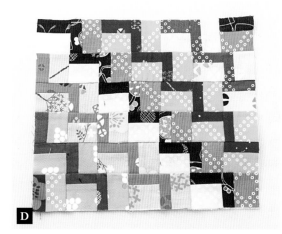

D

CUTTING for Tablet or Cell Phone Sleeve

Exterior	*Lining*	*Interfacing*
• Cut 1 Front.	• Cut 1 Front.	• Cut 1 Front.
• Cut 1 Back.	• Cut 1 Back.	• Cut 1 Back.
• Cut 1 Flap (from your interfaced patchwork or other exterior fabric).	• Cut 1 Flap.	• Cut 1 Flap (if you are not using patchwork for your flap).

Front and Back

1. Fuse the interfacing to the wrong side of the exterior pieces. (If you are using the flap patchwork, the interfacing has already been fused on.)

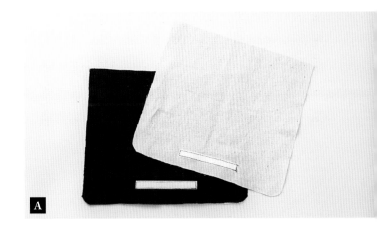

2. Attach the hook-and-loop tape onto the right sides of the front exterior and the flap lining, sewing around all 4 edges and backstitching at the beginning and end. **FIGURE A**

3. Place the front and back exterior pieces with right sides together. Sew around the side and bottom edges. Notch the rounded corner seams. Turn right side out and press. **FIGURE B**

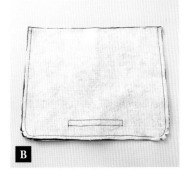

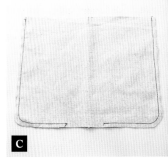

4. Repeat Step 3 using the front and back lining pieces; leave a 4″ opening for turning. Press the lining but leave it wrong side out. **FIGURE C**

Flap

1. Pin the piping around the side and bottom edges of the flap piece and stitch (see Adding Piping, page 12). Cut off the excess piping. **FIGURE D**

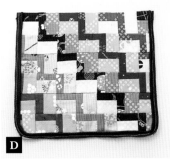

2. Pin the flap exterior to the flap lining with right sides together. Stitch only the sides and curved bottom edge seam, leaving the top edge unstitched. Stitch as close to the piping as possible, using a zipper foot on your machine if you have one. **FIGURE E**

3. Clip the curved seam. Turn right side out and press. **FIGURE F**

4. Center the flap onto the back piece of the sleeve with the exterior sides together, aligning the raw edges. Pin and baste in place. **FIGURE G**

5. Insert the exterior unit inside the lining with right sides together, sandwiching the flap between the exterior and the lining. Match the side seams of the exterior with the side seams of the lining as much as possible. **FIGURE H**

6. Pin the exterior and lining together around the opening of the sleeve. Sew around the opening. **FIGURE I**

7. Turn right side out through the opening left in the lining. Stitch the lining opening closed. Tuck the lining into the exterior. Press the top opening of the sleeve.

8. Topstitch around the opening ⅛″ from the edge.

F

G

H

I

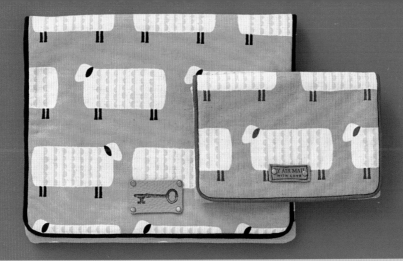

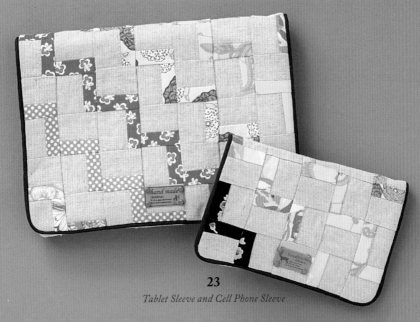

Tablet Sleeve and Cell Phone Sleeve

Scarlett Clutches

FINISHED SIZES: Rectangular: 17" wide × 8¼" high • Square: 14" wide × 12" high

The Scarlett Clutch includes a unique triangular patchwork design intended for the beginning sewist! The solid-color flaps make the tri-patchwork stand out with extra flair. Using two different sizes of triangles creates more style interest.

MATERIALS for Rectangular Clutch

15 different fat eighths for front, back, and flap exterior patchwork **OR** ⅝ yard of 44″-wide linen/cotton or quilting-weight cotton fabric for one-fabric exterior

¼ yard of solid fabric for flap bottom piece

⅔ yard for lining

1 yard of 20″-wide medium-weight fusible interfacing

16″ all-purpose zipper for clutch

6″ all-purpose zipper for zipper pocket

18 mm magnetic snap

MATERIALS for Square Clutch

15 different fat eighths for front, back, and flap exterior patchwork **OR** ⅝ yard of 44″-wide linen/cotton or quilting-weight cotton for one-fabric exterior

¼ yard of solid fabric for flap bottom piece

⅔ yard for lining

1¼ yards of 20″-wide medium-weight fusible interfacing

12″ all-purpose zipper for clutch

6″ all-purpose zipper for zipper pocket

18 mm magnetic snap

note

• *A ⅜″ seam allowance is included on the patterns.*

• *Backstitch at the beginning and end of each seam.*

Front, Back, and Flap Patchwork

- - - - - - - - - - - - - - - -

CUTTING for Rectangular Clutch

Fat eighths

• Cut 42 triangle A pieces using the Scarlett Clutches Triangle A pattern for front and back exterior (pullout page P1).

• Cut 38 triangle B pieces using the Scarlett Clutches Triangle B pattern for flap exterior (pullout page P1).

CUTTING for Square Clutch

Fat eighths

• Cut 40 triangle A pieces using the Scarlett Clutches Triangle A pattern for front and back exterior (pullout page P1).

• Cut 40 triangle B pieces using the Scarlett Clutches Triangle B pattern for flap exterior (pullout page P1).

note

A ¼˝ seam allowance is included for the patchwork.

- - - - - - - - - - - - - - - -

1. Arrange the A triangles (front and back) in rows (2 rows of 10 triangles and 2 rows of 11 triangles for the rectangular clutch; 5 rows of 8 triangles for the square clutch).

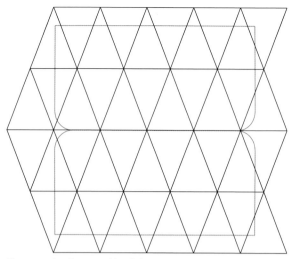

Rectangular front and back layout

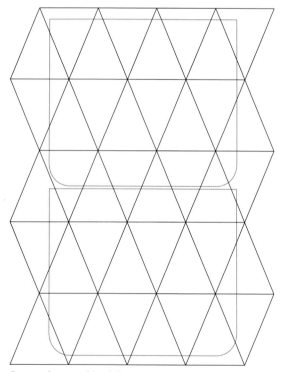

Square front and back layout

2. Match the edges of the first 2 triangles in the first row, right sides together, and sew. **FIGURE A**

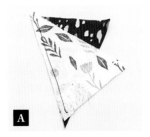

A

3. Add the next triangle and sew, keeping the edges matched as accurately as possible; then press. **FIGURE B**

4. Sew all the triangles into rows. **FIGURE C**

B

5. Sew the rows together and press. **FIGURE D**

6. Repeat Steps 1–5 for the B triangles for the flap patchwork (2 rows of 13 triangles and 1 row of 12 triangles for the rectangular clutch; 4 rows of 10 triangles for the square clutch).

C

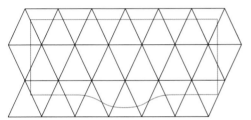

Rectangular flap layout

D

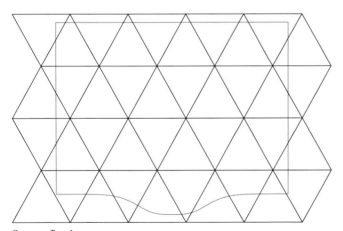

Square flap layout

Clutch Construction

Using either the Scarlett Clutches Front and Back (Rectangle), Scarlett Clutches Flap Top (Rectangle), Scarlett Clutches Flap Bottom (Rectangle), Scarlett Clutches Flap Lining (Rectangle), and Zipper Pocket patterns (pullout pages P1 and P2) **OR** the Scarlett Clutches Front and Back (Square), Scarlett Clutches Flap Top (Square), Scarlett Clutches Flap Bottom (Square), Scarlett Clutches Flap Lining (Square), and Zipper Pocket patterns (pullout pages P1 and P2), cut out the following pieces and transfer all points and references to the fabric.

CUTTING for Rectangular or Square Clutch

Exterior

- Cut 1 Front (from patchwork).
- Cut 1 Back (from patchwork).
- Cut 1 Flap Top (from patchwork or exterior fabric).
- Cut 1 Flap Bottom.
- Cut 2 pieces 2½″ × 1½″ for zipper ends.

Lining

- Cut 1 Front.
- Cut 1 Back.
- Cut 1 Flap Lining.
- Cut 2 Zipper Pockets.

Interfacing

- Cut 1 Front.
- Cut 1 Back.
- Cut 1 Flap Lining.

Lining Pocket

Make the lining pocket (see Zipper Pocket, page 10). FIGURE A

A

Flap

1. Stitch ⅛″ from the edge of the flap patchwork to secure the patchwork piecing. FIGURE B

B

2. Place the flap top and bottom pieces with right sides together, pin, and stitch. Clip the curves in the seam allowance (see Clipping and Trimming the Seam, page 7). FIGURE C

C

3. Press the seam toward the flap top and topstitch ⅛″ from the seam.

4. Fuse the interfacing onto the wrong side of the flap, following the manufacturer's instructions. Quilt by hand or machine. FIGURE D

D

5. Attach one side of the magnetic snap onto the flap lining and the other side of the snap to the front exterior (see Applying a Magnetic Snap, page 6).

6. Pin the flap exterior and flap lining with right sides together. Stitch only the sides and curved seam, leaving the straight edge at the top of the flap unstitched.

7. Clip the curved seam and turn it right side out. Press. If you wish, topstitch ¼˝ from the edges. **FIGURE E**

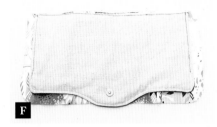

8. Fuse the interfacing onto the wrong side of the front and back exterior patchwork pieces, following the manufacturer's instructions. Quilt by hand or machine.

9. Center the flap onto the back piece of the clutch, with exterior sides together, aligning the raw edges. Pin and baste in place. **FIGURE F**

Install the Zipper

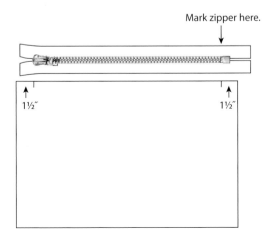

1. Fold 2 sides of the zipper end pieces ⅜˝ to the wrong side and press. Fold the piece in half widthwise, wrong sides together, and press to make a crease. **FIGURE G**

2. Measure in 1½˝ from each side at the top of the front exterior piece. Lay your zipper next to the top, with the opening end at a 1½˝ mark. Mark the zipper at the other 1½˝ mark.

Mark zipper here.

1½˝   1½˝

3. Unfold one side of a zipper end piece. Place the open end of the zipper onto the folded end of the zipper end piece and baste together. Refold the zipper end piece to enclose the end of the zipper. Topstitch ⅛″ from the seam. **FIGURE H**

4. To attach the other zipper end piece, baste the end piece where you marked the zipper, and then trim the excess zipper tape, leaving ½″. Then fold the end piece over and topstitch ⅛″ from the seam. **FIGURE I**

5. Pin the zipper to the top edge of the front exterior with right sides together. Center the zipper across the front. Stitch the panel and zipper using a zipper foot, sewing close to the tape edge. Backstitch to secure. **FIGURE J**

6. Pin the lining piece onto the zipper panel unit with the right side of the lining toward the right side of the exterior panel. The zipper will now be between the exterior and the lining. Sew the zipper close to the coils. Backstitch on both ends. **FIGURE K**

7. After sewing the zipper, flip the lining toward the interior with wrong sides together and press. Topstitch the exterior and lining close to the zipper. **FIGURE L**

8. Repeat Steps 5–7 to attach the other exterior and lining pieces to the second side of the zipper. **FIGURE M**

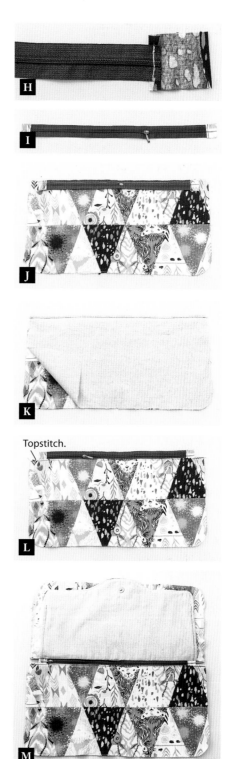

H

I

J

K

Topstitch.

L

M

Exterior and Lining

1. Match the front and back exterior, right sides together, with the flap between the 2 exterior pieces; then match the front and back lining, right sides together. Open the zipper partway. (It's very difficult to turn right side out when the zipper is closed.) Pin and sew all the way around the clutch. Leave a 4˝ opening on the bottom of the lining to turn it right side out.

2. Clip the curved seams and trim the overlapping seams (see Clipping and Trimming the Seam, page 7).

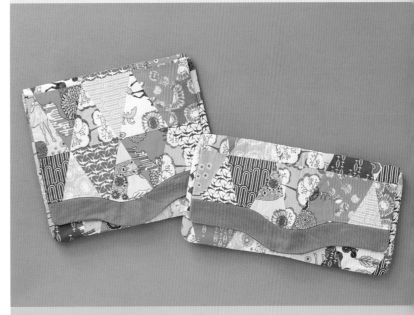

3. Turn the clutch right side out and tuck the lining inside the bag. Stitch the opening in the lining closed and press.

Elegant Frame Purse

The Elegant Frame Purse is a beautiful bag that can be designed to go well with any outfit. This pattern uses a simple stitch-and-flip quilting method to make the front and back exterior. A resin frame that uses screws to hold it in place is easy to attach to the bag. The Elegant Frame Purse makes the perfect gift or is simply a great purse for yourself!

MATERIALS

1 strip 1½″ × 16″ of each of 12 different fabrics for front and back exterior patchwork **OR** ¼ yard of 44″-wide linen/cotton, home decor, or quilting-weight cotton fabric for one-fabric exterior

¼ yard for gusset exterior

⅜ yard of 44″-wide quilting-weight cotton for lining

¼ yard of 20″-wide medium-weight fusible interfacing for gusset

⅝ yard of 20″-wide medium-weight nonfusible interfacing

1¼ yards of coordinating piping

10″ × 4″ wood or resin purse frame with screws

6″ all-purpose zipper for zipper pocket

Fabric glue (optional)

Scraps of thin leather, about ½″ × ½″ for each screw hole in your purse frame

note
• *A ¼″ seam allowance is included for the patchwork.*

• *A ⅜″ seam allowance is included on the patterns.*

• *Backstitch at the beginning and end of each seam.*

Patchwork

1. Lay out the strips in the design you want.

2. Cut a piece of nonfusible interfacing 14″ × 16″. Place the first strip near one long edge of the interfacing, right side up. **FIGURE A**

3. Place the second strip on top of the first strip, with right sides together. Stitch along the long side, through all layers, on the edge farthest away from the edge of the interfacing. **FIGURE B**

4. Flip the strip open and press. **FIGURE C**

5. Attach the third strip in the same manner. **FIGURE D**

6. Repeat this process for the remaining strips. Quilt by hand or machine. **FIGURE E**

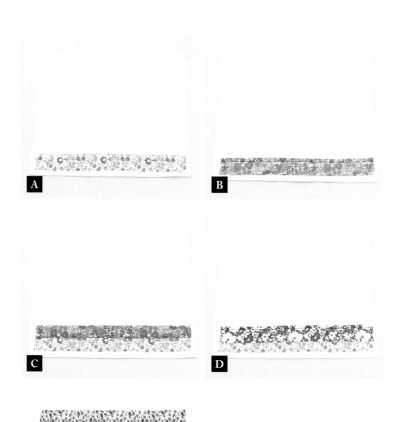

Purse Construction

Using the Elegant Frame Purse Front and Back, Elegant Frame Purse Gusset, and Zipper Pocket patterns (pullout page P2), cut out the following pieces and transfer all points and references to the fabric.

- - - - - - - - - - - - - - -

CUTTING

Exterior

• Cut 1 Front (from patchwork or exterior fabric).

• Cut 1 Back (from patchwork or exterior fabric).

Gusset fabric

• Cut 1 Gusset.

Lining

• Cut 1 Front.

• Cut 1 Back.

• Cut 1 Gusset.

• Cut 2 Zipper Pockets.

Fusible Interfacing

• Cut 1 Gusset.

- - - - - - - - - - - - - - -

Exterior and Lining

1. Sew ⅛˝ from the edges around the outside of the front and back pieces to secure your patchwork.

2. Attach the piping onto the front and back exterior pieces (see Adding Piping, page 12). **FIGURE A**

A

3. Fuse the interfacing to the wrong side of the gusset, following the manufacturer's instructions.

4. Place the front and gusset exterior pieces right sides together. Pin the center and top points first, then pin the rest of the seam, clipping the curved seam if needed. Stitch the pinned seam. **FIGURE B**

B

5. Pin and sew the back exterior piece to the gusset piece in the same manner. Turn the exterior right side out. **FIGURE C**

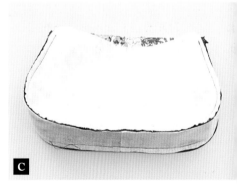

C

6. Make the lining zipper pocket (see Zipper Pocket, page 10). **FIGURE D**

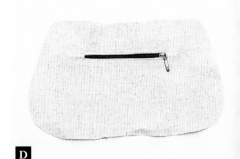

D

7. Repeat Steps 4 and 5 for attaching the front and back lining to the gusset lining. Leave a 4″ opening for turning on one bottom seam. Leave the lining with the wrong sides out. **FIGURE E**

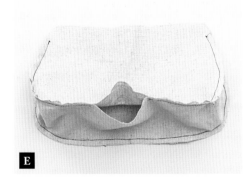

E

8. Tuck the exterior into the lining with right sides together. **FIGURE F**

9. Pin and sew around the top opening of the bag. Clip and trim the seams (see Clipping and Trimming the Seam, page 7). Turn the bag right side out through the opening in the lining seam; stitch the opening closed. **FIGURE G**

F

10. Tuck the lining into the exterior. Press and topstitch ⅛″ from the seam around the top of the bag. **FIGURE H**

G

H

Attach the Purse Frame

1. If you want to apply the fabric glue for extra sturdiness, apply fabric glue on the lip of the purse—but this type of frame doesn't need glue.

2. Use a washable marker to mark the top center of the purse. Then use a sharp tool to push the purse into the channel of the frame. Make sure to align the center of the bag with the center of the frame. Then push in the sides one at a time.

3. After aligning the bag correctly, push in a small amount of leather right below the screw hole. Then plug in the screw; however, don't tighten the screw yet. Repeat for the rest of the holes. Also repeat the process for the other side of the purse opening. When the overall shape of the bag is to your liking, tighten the screws.

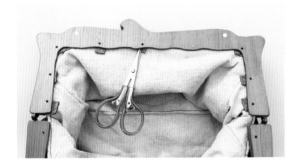

Isabella Bag

Finished size: 16" wide × 13" high (without the handle)

The patchwork for this bag is simple squares sewn together. The front pockets allow for easy storage of light and small items, but you can make the bag even easier for a beginner by choosing not to include the front pockets. The zipper pocket on the inside is perfect to store keys or makeup. With its attractive appearance and its equally practical design, the Isabella Bag is a must-have for any collection!

MATERIALS

29 squares 6¼″ × 6¼″ of 6–9 different fabrics for front and back, **OR** 1 yard of 44″-wide heavy-weight home decorator or quilting-weight cotton for one-fabric exterior

1 piece of coordinating fabric 4″ × 14½″ for front pocket gussets

1 yard for lining

1¼ yards of 20″-wide medium-weight fusible interfacing

6″ all-purpose zipper for lining pocket

2 magnetic snaps, 18 mm

2 O-rings, 2½″

3″ of 1″-wide hook-and-loop tape (nonfusible)

2 decorative buttons, 1″ (optional)

note

• *A ¼″ seam allowance is included for the patchwork.*

• *A ⅜″ seam allowance is included on the patterns.*

• *Backstitch at the beginning and end of each seam.*

Exterior Patchwork

1. Arrange the 29 blocks into 4 rows of 7 blocks each plus 1 extra in the upper right corner.

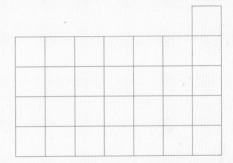

2. Sew the blocks into vertical rows.

3. Sew the rows together and press.

Bag Construction

Using the Isabella Bag Front and Back, Isabella Bag Flap, Isabella Bag Pocket, and Isabella Bag Pocket Flap patterns (pullout page P1), cut out the following pieces and transfer all points and references to the fabric.

CUTTING

Exterior

(from patchwork or exterior fabric)

• Cut 1 Front.

• Cut 1 Back.

• Cut 2 Pocket Flaps.

• Cut 2 Pockets.

• Cut 1 Flap.

• Cut 1 piece 5¼″ × 15″ for strap.

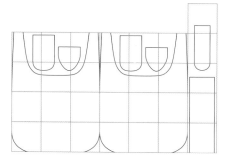

Front pocket gussets

(from coordinating fabric)

• Cut 2 pieces 1½″ × 14½″.

Lining

• Cut 1 Front.

• Cut 1 Back.

• Cut 1 Flap.

• Cut 2 Pocket Flaps.

• Cut 2 pieces 6¾″ × 12″ for standard lining pocket.

• Cut 2 Zipper Pockets.

Interfacing

• Cut 1 Front.

• Cut 1 Back.

Exterior

1. Fuse the interfacing on the wrong side of the front and back patchwork pieces, following the manufacturer's instructions.

2. Quilt by hand or machine.

Pockets

1. Cut the hook-and-loop tape into 2 pieces, each 1″ long. Place the rough side of 1 piece onto the right side of a pocket flap lining, and place the soft side on the right side of the pocket. Sew in a rectangular shape, backstitching at both ends. **FIGURE A**

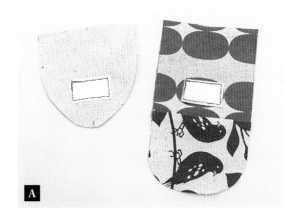

2. Pin the pocket piece to the gusset piece with right sides facing. First, match the center of the pocket bottom and the center of the gusset; then pin the rest in place. Stitch the gusset and the pocket pieces. Clip the gusset piece only as necessary to help ease it around the curve of the pocket piece. Stitch around the edge of the gusset to prevent raveling, using an overlock or zigzag stitch if you can. **FIGURE B**

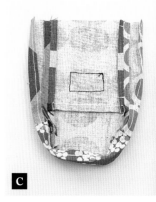

3. Flip the pocket piece wrong side up and press the long edge of the gusset in ⅜″, wrong sides together. **FIGURE C**

4. Fold in the top edge of the pocket ½″, fold it in again, and pin. Topstitch ⅛″ from the inner folded edge. Repeat Steps 1–4 to make the second front pocket. **FIGURE D**

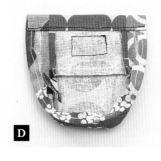
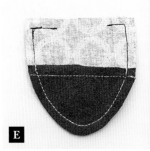

5. Pin a pocket flap and a pocket flap lining piece right sides together. Stitch all the way around, leaving some space for turning. **FIGURE E**

6. Clip and trim the curved seams (see Clipping and Trimming the Seam, page 7). Turn the flap right sides out. **FIGURE F**

7. Topstitch ¼″ from the seam. Repeat Steps 5–7 to make the second pocket flap. **FIGURE G**

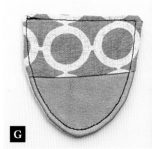

Exterior

1. Pin the pocket flap to the bag front where indicated on the pattern with the right side of the flap facing the right side of the bag, as shown. Stitch ⅛″ from the straight edge of the flap, backstitching at each end. **FIGURE A**

2. Pin the pocket to the front piece as indicated on the pattern, so the top of the pocket is up against the bottom edge of the flap. Topstitch ⅛″ from the folded edge of the gusset, backstitching at each top corner of the pocket. Follow Steps 1 and 2 to attach the other pocket. **FIGURE B**

3. Attach the female side of the magnetic snap onto the right side of the front exterior piece (see Applying a Magnetic Snap, page 6). **FIGURE C**

4. With the front exterior piece wrong side up, fold each dart with right sides together, matching the dart lines. Pin and stitch along the dart lines, backstitching at the beginning and end. **FIGURE D**

5. Press the darts toward the bottom edge. Stitch darts in the back exterior piece the same way, but press the darts toward the sides.

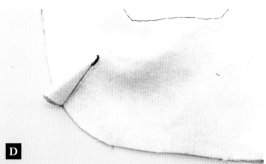

6. Pin the front and back exterior pieces with right sides together. Stitch all the way around the outside of the bag, backstitching on both ends. **FIGURE E**

7. Clip the curved seams.

Stitch the Flap

1. Attach the male side of the magnetic snap onto the right side of the flap lining. **FIGURE F**

2. Pin the flap exterior and the flap lining with right sides together. Stitch the long curved edge of the flap, backstitching on both ends. Leave the top opening unstitched. Clip the curved seam (See Clipping and Trimming the Seam, page 7). **FIGURE G**

3. Turn the flap right side out. Press and topstitch ¼″ from the edge. **FIGURE H**

4. Position the flap on the back piece of the bag with exterior right sides together. Baste the flap and bag together. **FIGURE I**

E

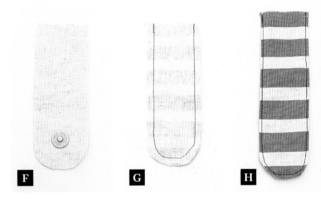

F   G   H

I

Lining

1. Make the lining pocket and position it on the front lining piece 4½˝ down from the top (see Standard Pocket, page 8). Stitch the pocket to the lining and sew the pocket divider lines as desired. **FIGURE J**

2. Stitch the zipper pocket on the back lining piece (see Zipper Pocket, page 10).

3. Attach 1 piece of a magnetic snap to the right side of the front lining, and the other piece to the right side of the back lining, where indicated on the pattern (see Applying a Magnetic Snap, page 6). **FIGURE K**

4. Repeat Steps 4–7 of the Exterior section (page 42) to assemble the lining. Leave a 6˝ opening for turning. **FIGURE L**

J

K

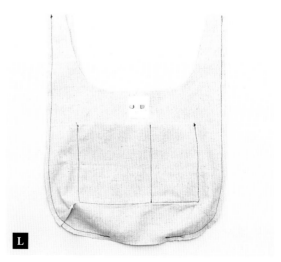

L

Assemble the Bag

1. Press the exterior and lining seams open. Turn the exterior right side out. Place the exterior into the lining with right sides together. **FIGURE M**

2. Pin and sew the exterior and lining together all the way around the opening and the handles. **FIGURE N**

3. Clip the curved seam and trim the corner seams (see Clipping and Trimming the Seam, page 7).

4. Turn the bag right side out through the opening in the lining. Push out the handle corners using a turning tool or capped pen. Stitch the lining opening closed.

Finish the Bag

1. Tuck the lining inside the exterior. Press the handles and opening of the bag. Topstitch ⅛˝ from the edge. **FIGURE O**

2. Insert the bag handle extension through the O-ring; fold the bag handle extension over 1½˝ to the lining side. Pin and sew, backstitching several times at both the beginning and the end. Repeat this process for the other bag handle extension. **FIGURE P**

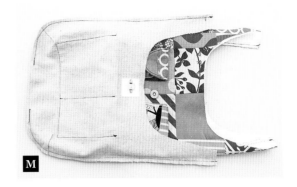

M

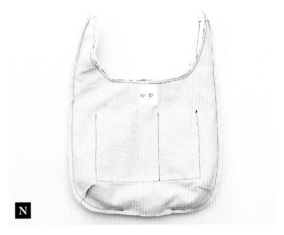

N

O

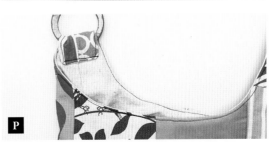

P

3. Make the strap (see Strap C, page 14). Topstitch along all edges of the strap.

4. Insert one end of the strap through an O-ring; fold the strap over 1½″ to the lining side. Pin and sew, backstitching several times at both the beginning and the end. Repeat this process for the other end of the strap.

Chloe Bag

This handy, trendy bag includes simple strip piecing for the front. The lining zipper pocket provides a small but practical compartment to securely store your belongings. Make this stylish and fashionable bag for someone special today!

MATERIALS for Large Bag

14 strips 2″ × 25″ from various fabrics **OR** ½ yard of 44″-wide quilting-weight cotton, home decor, or linen/cotton for one-fabric exterior including gusset, strap, and loops

¼ yard of exterior fabric for gusset, strap, and loops if you are using patchwork for the front and back of the bag

½ yard for lining

⅜ yard of 44″-wide fusible fleece interfacing

12″ all-purpose zipper

2 square 1″ rings

6″ all-purpose zipper for zipper pocket

2 yards of ½″ double-fold bias tape

MATERIALS for Small Bag

14 strips 1½″ × 17″ from various fabrics **OR** ⅜ yard of 44″-wide quilting-weight cotton, home decor, or linen/cotton for one-fabric exterior including gusset, strap, and loops

¼ yard of exterior fabric for gusset, strap, and loops if you are using patchwork for the front and back of the bag

½ yard for lining

¼ yard of 44″-wide fusible fleece interfacing

8″ all-purpose zipper

2 square ¾″ rings

6″ all-purpose zipper for zipper pocket

1½ yards of ½″ double-fold bias tape

note

• *A ¼″ seam allowance is included for the patchwork.*

• *A ⅜″ seam allowance is included on the patterns.*

• *Backstitch at the beginning and end of each seam.*

Patchwork

Sew 7 of the strips together and press. Repeat this step with the remaining 7 strips.

Bag Construction

Using either the Chloe Bag (Large) Front and Back Exterior, Chloe Bag (Large) Front and Back, Chloe Bag (Large) Gusset, and Zipper Pocket patterns (pullout page P2) **OR** the Chloe Bag (Small) Front and Back Exterior, Chloe Bag (Small) Front and Back, Chloe Bag (Small) Gusset, and Zipper Pocket patterns (pullout page P2), cut out the following pieces and transfer all points and references to the fabric.

- -

CUTTING for Large or Small Bag

Exterior

• Cut 4 (2 and 2 reversed) Front and Back Exterior (from patchwork or exterior fabric).

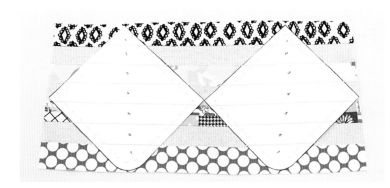

• Cut 1 Gusset.

• Cut 2 pieces 1½″ × 2¾″ for zipper ends for large bag.

• Cut 2 pieces 1½″ × 2¾″ for zipper ends for small bag.

Exterior, continued

• Cut 2 pieces 2″ × 3″ for loop.

• Cut 1 piece 2″ × 44″ for strap.

Lining

• Cut 1 Front.

• Cut 1 Back.

• Cut 1 Gusset.

• Cut 2 Zipper Pockets.

Interfacing

• Cut 1 Front.

• Cut 1 Back.

• Cut 1 Gusset.

Bag Exterior

1. Place the 2 front exterior pieces with right sides together; pin and stitch the center seam. Press. **FIGURES A & B**

2. Repeat Step 1 to make the back piece.

3. Fuse the interfacing onto the wrong side of the patchwork, following the manufacturer's instructions. Quilt by hand or machine.

Lining

Make the lining zipper pocket (see Zipper Pocket, page 10). **FIGURE C**

Bag Zipper

1. Attach the zipper end pieces. (See Scarlett Clutches, Install the Zipper, Steps 1–4, page 29.) Measure in 1˝ from each side at the top of the front exterior piece (instead of 1½˝) for this bag. **FIGURE D**

2. Lay the zipper on the front exterior piece with right sides together. You will be able to see the wrong side of the zipper. Pin the zipper in place. Stitch together using a zipper foot, sewing close to the zipper tape edge and leaving the ⅜˝ seam allowance unsewn on both ends. Backstitch to secure. **FIGURE E**

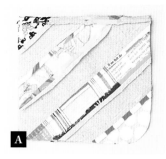

A

B

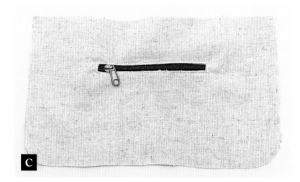

C

D

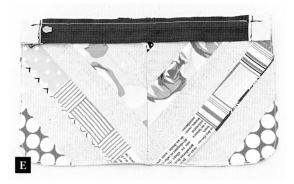

E

3. Pin the lining piece onto the zipper with the right side toward the right side of the exterior piece. The zipper will now be between the exterior and the lining. Sew the zipper close to the coils, leave the ⅜″ seam allowance unsewn on both ends. Backstitch at both ends. **FIGURE F**

4. After sewing the zipper with the lining, flip the lining toward the exterior, so the wrong sides are together, and press. Topstitch all three layers (exterior, zipper, and lining) from the outside, leaving the ⅜″ seam allowance unsewn on both ends. **FIGURE G**

5. Baste the front exterior and lining pieces together around the sides and bottom.

6. Follow Steps 2–5 to attach the back exterior and lining pieces to the zipper in the same manner. **FIGURE H**

Bag Body

1. Make the loop pieces (see Strap B, page 14).

2. Fuse the interfacing to the wrong side of the gusset exterior. Place the gusset exterior and gusset lining with wrong sides together and baste all the way around. Pin the loops onto the short ends of the right side of the gusset and baste. **FIGURE I**

F

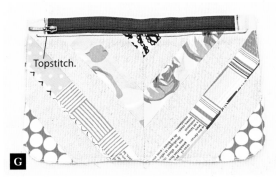

Topstitch.

G

H

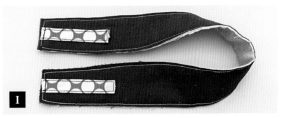

I

3. Pin the gusset piece to the front piece with right sides together. Stitch the bag using a ⅜″ seam allowance around the sides and bottom, making a U shape and backstitching on both ends. Leave a ⅜″ seam allowance unsewn at both ends. Unzip the bag zipper halfway. **FIGURE J**

4. Repeat Step 3 to attach the gusset to the back piece. **FIGURE K**

5. Pin and sew the zipper end piece and gusset piece together, sandwiching the loop between the gusset and zipper end piece. Backstitch at both ends. Repeat this step for the other side of the gusset. **FIGURE L**

6. Unfold the length of bias binding. Fold and press one short end of the bias binding under ⅜″. Beginning at the bottom center of the back, pin the raw edge of the bias binding to the outside edge of the bag, right sides together. Pin all the way around, lapping the end of the bias binding over the folded end ⅜″. **FIGURE M**

J

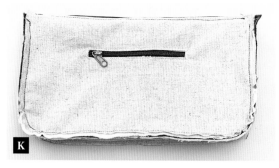

K

L

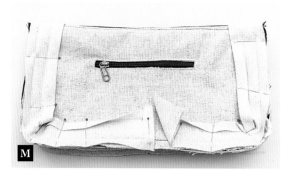

M

7. Stitch the bias strip to the seam allowance all the way around the bag. **FIGURE N**

8. Fold the bias over, encasing the seam. Topstitch on the bias tape, following the first sewing line. Then turn the bag right side out through the zipper. **FIGURE O**

Strap

1. Make the strap (see Strap C, page 14). **FIGURE P**

2. Insert a ring onto the loop piece. Fold the loop piece over the ring and pin. Stitch back and forth across the loop to securely hold the ring in place. **FIGURE Q**

3. Insert the strap into the ring. Fold the strap over the ring and pin. Stitch several times over the strap for strength. Repeat Steps 2 and 3 for the other side. **FIGURE R**

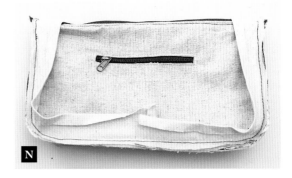

N

O

P

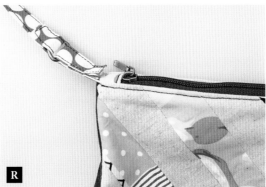

Q

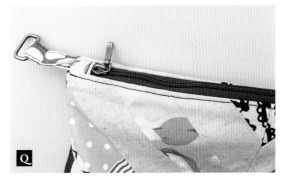

R

Tailynn Bag

Finished size: 17″ wide × 15½″ high × 3″ deep

From a beach bag to a diaper bag, this bag really is practical! The diagonal patchwork blocks give it a simple, yet elegant, design. Choose a beautiful array of colors to make it uniquely your own.

MATERIALS

note
If you want a scrappy look for the patchwork blocks, cut a total of 16 strips 2¼″ × width of fabric (or 32 strips 2¼″ × 18″ if using fat quarters) from a variety of fabrics.

4 different fat quarters **OR** ⅝ yard of 44″-wide linen/cotton or quilting-weight cotton fabric for one-fabric exterior

⅜ yard of 44″-wide fabric for gusset

1⅛ yards of 44″-wide quilting-weight cotton for lining

1¾ yards of 20″-wide medium-weight fusible interfacing

8 sheets of plain paper at least 9½″ × 9½″

1 pair of sew-on leather handles (1″ × 20½″)

18 mm magnetic snap

6″ all-purpose zipper for lining pocket

⅝ yard of ½″-wide elastic for lining pocket

note
• *A ¼″ seam allowance is included for the patchwork.*

• *A ⅜″ seam allowance is included on the patterns.*

• *Backstitch at the beginning and end of each seam.*

Patchwork

CUTTING

Fat quarters
• Cut 8 strips 2¼″ × 18″ from each fat quarter.

1. Cut a piece of paper to 9½″ square. With a pencil, draw a diagonal line from corner to corner. Using a ruler, draw additional diagonal lines 1¾″ apart and parallel to the centerline.

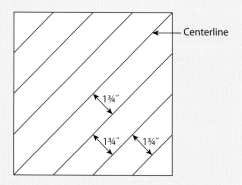

2. Place one end of the first strip right side up at the corner of the square and overlapping a diagonal line by ¼". Pin it in place and trim off the excess. Be sure it covers the paper completely. **FIGURE A**

3. Add a second strip with right sides facing and pin in place. **FIGURE B**

4. Set the stitch length on your machine to 1.8 (smaller than for normal piecing). Stitch through all layers using a ¼" seam allowance. Flip the fabric strip toward the paper, right side up, and press. Trim off the excess. **FIGURE C**

5. Repeat Steps 3 and 4 to attach the remaining strips. **FIGURE D**

6. Flip the block over and press again.

7. Trim the block to 9½" × 9½". **FIGURE E**

8. Repeat Steps 1–7 to make a total of 8 blocks. Carefully remove the paper from the blocks.

9. Sew 4 blocks into 2 rows of 2 blocks each. Press. Sew the 2 rows together. Press. Repeat with the remaining 4 blocks. **FIGURE F**

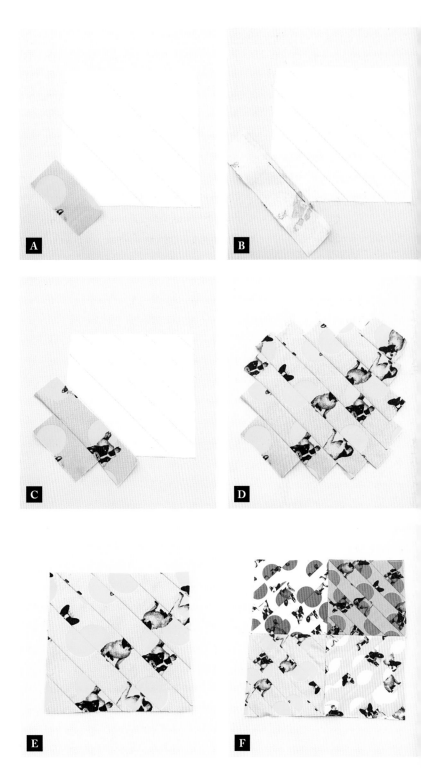

Bag Construction

CUTTING

Using the Tailynn Bag Front and Back and Zipper Pocket patterns (pullout page P2), cut out the following pieces and transfer all points and references to the fabric.

Exterior

- Cut 1 Front (from patch-work or exterior fabric).
- Cut 1 Back (from patch-work or exterior fabric).
- Cut 2 pieces 3¾″ × 23⅞″ for Gusset.

Lining

- Cut 1 Front.
- Cut 1 Back.
- Cut 2 pieces 3¾″ × 23⅞″ for gusset.
- Cut 1 Elastic Pocket (see Elastic Pocket, page 9).
- Cut 2 Zipper Pockets.

Interfacing

- Cut 1 Front.
- Cut 1 Back.
- Cut 2 pieces 3¾″ × 23⅞″ for gusset.

Exterior

1. Fuse the interfacing onto the wrong side of the front and back exterior pieces and the gusset pieces, following the manufacturer's instructions. Quilt by hand or machine.

2. Match the gusset exterior pieces with right sides together. Stitch together along one short edge and press. Topstitch on each side ⅛″ from the seam for reinforcement.

3. Pin the front exterior piece to the assembled gusset with right sides together. First, match the center front with the gusset seam. Then stitch the gusset and the front together. **FIGURE A**

4. Repeat Step 3 to attach the back exterior piece to the gusset. **FIGURE B**

5. Clip the curved seams. Turn the bag right side out. (See Clipping and Trimming the Seam, page 7).

Lining

1. Sew the lining zipper pocket (see Zipper Pocket, page 10). **FIGURE C**

2. Sew the lining elastic pocket (see Elastic Pocket, page 9).

3. Apply a magnetic snap to the front and back lining where indicated on the pattern (see Applying a Magnetic Snap, page 6). **FIGURE D**

4. Repeat Exterior, Steps 2–4 (previous page) for assembling the lining. Leave 5″ unstitched along one gusset seam for turning. **FIGURE E**

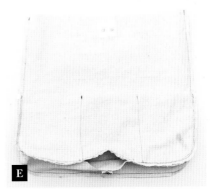

Assembly

1. Insert the exterior into the lining, right sides together. **FIGURE A**

2. Pin the exterior and lining together around the opening of the bag. Stitch. **FIGURE B**

3. Trim off the overlapped seams.

4. Turn the bag right side out. Pin the opening in the lining and sew it closed.

5. Tuck the lining into the exterior. Press the top opening of the bag. Topstitch around the opening ¼″ from the edge. **FIGURE C**

6. Attach the sew-on leather handles. Place the handle on the exterior of the bag at the desired location. Stitch the handle by hand using a running stitch and doubled thread, sewing so that the thread does not show in the space between every other hole. **FIGURES D & E**

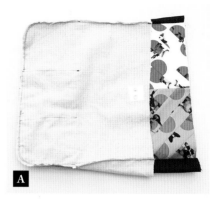

A

C

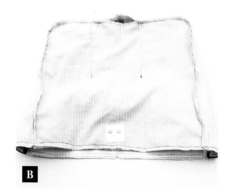

B

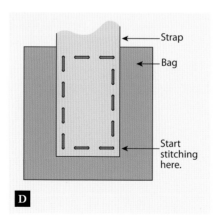

Strap

Bag

Start stitching here.

D

E

7. Use a running stitch over the handle a second time, alternating so that the thread fills the space between every other hole.

Glenda Boston Bag and Pouch

FINISHED SIZES: Bag: 16" wide × 16" high × 4" deep • **Pouch:** 11" wide × 5½" high × 1¾" deep

This Boston Bag and Pouch set is made with Log Cabin–style patchwork. Making a Log Cabin block may look complicated, but this method is actually very simple. Because the bag is large and spacious, it can be used as a travel bag or even a diaper bag!

MATERIALS for Bag

2½ yards of 44″-wide linen/cotton, home decor, or quilting-weight cotton fabric for exterior patchwork **OR** 1 yard of 44″-wide fabric for one-fabric exterior

note

If you want a scrappy look for the Log Cabin blocks, cut 1¼″-wide strips from a variety of fabrics.

1 yard of 44″-wide quilting-weight cotton for lining

4 yards of ½″ double-fold bias tape for binding seams

1¾ yards of 20″-wide lightweight fusible interfacing

27″ all-purpose zipper

6″ all-purpose zipper for lining pocket

⅝ yard of ⅜″-wide elastic for lining pocket

1 pair of sew-on leather handles (1″ × 20½″)

4 yards piping (optional)

MATERIALS for Pouch

1 yard of 44″-wide linen/cotton, home decor, or quilting-weight cotton fabric for patchwork exterior and straps **OR** ½ yard of 44″-wide fabric for one-fabric exterior.

½ yard of 44″-wide quilting-weight cotton for lining

2 yards of ½″ double-fold bias tape for binding seams

½ yard of 20″-wide lightweight fusible interfacing

16″ all-purpose zipper

2 yards piping (optional)

note

• *A ¼″ seam allowance is included for the patchwork.*

• *A ⅜″ seam allowance is included on the patterns.*

• *Backstitch at the beginning and end of each seam.*

Patchwork

CUTTING for Bag

- Cut 32 squares 1¼″ × 1¼″.

- Cut strips 1¼″ × fabric width.
  (Cut the strips as you need them.)

CUTTING for Pouch

- Cut 10 squares 1¼″ × 1¼″.

- Cut strips 1¼″ × fabric width.
  (Cut the strips as you need them.)

----

1. Align a 1¼″ square with the end of a strip with right sides together. Stitch along one side of the square and trim the strip to match the square. **FIGURE A**

2. Press open.

3. Place the strip on top of the pieced unit with right sides together. Pin and sew as shown, backstitching on both ends. Trim off the remaining strip. **FIGURE B**

4. Press open. **FIGURE C**

5. Place the strip on the top edge of the pieced unit again. Pin and sew, trim off remaining strip, and press open. **FIGURE D**

6. Add another strip and press open. **FIGURES E & F**

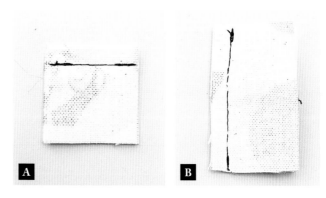

A

B

C

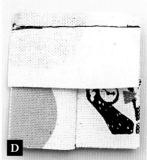

D

E

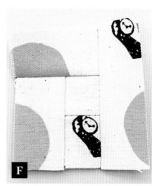

F

note
Add the strips clockwise around the block, backstitching on both ends of each seam.

7. Repeat this process until the block is approximately 7″ × 7″. Trim the block to 6¾″ × 6¾″.

8. Make 32 blocks for the bag or 10 blocks for the pouch.

9. For the bag, arrange the blocks into one section 3 blocks × 6 blocks (bag front and back) and one section 2 blocks × 7 blocks (bag zipper panels and gusset). For the pouch, arrange the blocks into one section 2 blocks × 2 blocks (pouch front and back) and one section 2 blocks × 3 blocks (pouch zipper panels and gusset).

10. Sew the blocks into rows. Press. **FIGURE G**

11. Sew the rows together. Press.

Construction

Using either the Glenda Boston Bag Front and Back and Zipper Pocket patterns (pullout page P2) **OR** the Glenda Boston Pouch Front and Back patterns (pullout page P1), cut out the following pieces and transfer all points and references to the fabric.

- -

CUTTING for Bag

Exterior

• Cut 1 Front (from patchwork or exterior fabric).

• Cut 1 Back (from patchwork or exterior fabric).

• Cut 2 pieces 2½″ × 27″ for zipper panels (from patchwork or exterior fabric).

• Cut 2 pieces 4¾″ × 18½″ for gusset (from patchwork or exterior fabric).

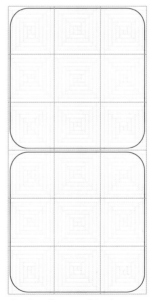

Cut bag front and back.

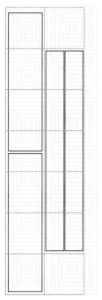

Cut zipper panel and gusset pieces.

Lining

- Cut 1 Front.
- Cut 1 Back.
- Cut 2 pieces 2½˝ × 27˝ for zipper panels.
- Cut 2 pieces 4¾˝ × 18½˝ for gusset.
- Cut 2 Zipper Pockets.
- Cut 1 Elastic Pocket (see Elastic Pocket, page 9).

Interfacing

- Cut 1 Front.
- Cut 1 Back.
- Cut 2 pieces 2½˝ × 27˝ for zipper panels.
- Cut 2 pieces 4¾˝ × 18½˝ for gusset.

CUTTING for Pouch

Exterior

- Cut 1 Front (from patchwork or exterior fabric).
- Cut 1 Back (from patchwork or exterior fabric).
- Cut 2 pieces 1¼˝ × 15¼˝ for zipper panel.
- Cut 2 pieces 2½˝ × 9½˝ for gusset.
- Cut 2 pieces 2½˝ × 9˝ for handles.

Lining

- Cut 1 Front.
- Cut 1 Back.
- Cut 2 pieces 1¼˝ × 15¼˝ for zipper panel.
- Cut 2 pieces 2½˝ × 9½˝ for gusset.

Interfacing

- Cut 1 Front.
- Cut 1 Back.
- Cut 2 pieces 1¼˝ × 15¼˝ for zipper panel.
- Cut 2 pieces 2½˝ × 9½˝ for gusset.

Bag Exterior and Lining

1. Fuse the interfacing onto the wrong side of the front, back, zipper panel, and gusset exterior pieces, following the manufacturer's instructions. Quilt by hand or machine. Add piping around the edge of the front and back pieces, if desired (see Adding Piping, page 12).

2. Attach the lining zipper pocket (see Zipper Pocket, page 10).

3. Stitch the elastic pocket (see Elastic Pocket, page 9). **FIGURE A**

4. Pin the front exterior and front lining pieces with wrong sides together. Baste around the outside edges. Repeat with the back exterior and back lining pieces.

A

Bag Zipper Panels and Gusset Panel

1. Install the zipper (see Scarlett Clutches, Install the Zipper, Steps 5–8, page 30) using the zipper panel exterior and zipper panel lining pieces. **FIGURE B**

2. Pin the 2 gusset exterior pieces at one short end, right sides together. Stitch. Press the seam open. Join the 2 gusset lining pieces the same way.

3. Pin the gusset exterior piece to the gusset lining piece, wrong sides together, and baste all the way around. Pin the ends of the assembled zipper panel to the ends of the gusset piece to form a ring, exterior sides together. Stitch the seams. **FIGURE C**

4. Unfold a 5″ length of bias binding (2½″ for the pouch). Pin the binding to the zipper panel/gusset seam, matching raw edges and with right sides together.

5. Stitch along the crease line closest to the edge of the trimmed seam, backstitching at both ends. Fold the binding over to encase the raw edge and pin.

6. Topstitch the binding, ⅛″ from the inner fold of the binding, through all layers. **FIGURE D**

7. Repeat Steps 4–6 for the other seam.

Bag Assembly

1. Fold the zipper/gusset piece to find and mark the centers of the zipper panel and the gusset. Pin the zipper/gusset piece to the front, exterior sides together, matching the zipper/gusset piece centers to the front centers and the zipper/gusset piece seams to seam markings on the front. Stitch all the way around the front of the bag. Clip the zipper/gusset piece only as necessary to help ease it around the curve of the front piece. Unzip the zipper halfway. **FIGURE E**

2. Repeat Step 1 to attach the zipper/gusset piece to the bag back piece. **FIGURE F**

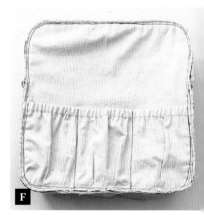

Add Bias Binding to Bag

1. Unfold one 64″ length of bias binding (35″ for the pouch). Fold and press one short end of the bias binding under ⅜″. Beginning at the bottom center, pin the raw edge of the bias binding to the outside edge of the bag, with right sides together. Pin all the way around, lapping the end of the bias binding over the folded end ⅜″. **FIGURE G**

2. Stitch along the crease line closest to the outside edge. Fold the binding over to encase the raw edge and pin.

3. Topstitch the binding ⅛″ from the inner fold of the binding, through all layers. Repeat Steps 1–3 to attach the binding to other side of the gusset. Turn the bag right side out and press. **FIGURE H**

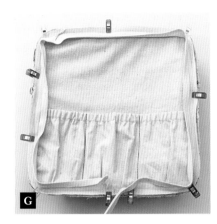

G

Attach the Bag Handle

1. Attach the leather/webbing handle. Place the handle on the exterior of the bag at the desired location. Use a running stitch to attach the handle to the bag, sewing so that the thread does not show in the space between every other hole. (See Tailynn Bag, Assembly, Steps 6 and 7, page 60.)

2. Stitch over the handle a second time with a running stitch, alternating so that the thread fills the space between every other hole.

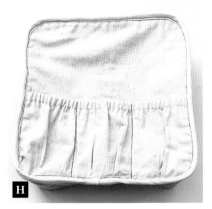

H

Pouch Assembly

Zipper Panels and Gusset

1. Fuse the interfacing onto the wrong side of the exterior pieces, following the manufacturer's instructions. Quilt by hand or machine.

2. Pin the front exterior and front lining pieces with wrong sides together. Baste around the outside edges. Repeat with the back exterior and back lining pieces.

3. Follow the instructions in Bag Zipper Panels and Gusset Panel, Steps 1–7 (page 67), to prepare the zipper and gusset.

Pouch Handles

1. Sew the handles (see Strap A, page 14).

2. Pin the handles onto the right sides of the front and back pieces as shown, and baste in place.

Bag Assembly

1. Fold the zipper/gusset piece to find and mark the centers of the zipper panel and the gusset. Pin the zipper/gusset piece to the front, exterior sides together, matching the zipper/gusset piece centers to the front centers and the zipper/gusset piece seams to seam markings on the front. Stitch all the way around the front of the bag. Stitch again over the handles to secure them. Clip the zipper/gusset piece only as necessary to help ease it around the curve of the front piece.

2. Unzip the zipper halfway. Repeat Step 1 to attach the zipper/gusset piece to the bag back piece.

3. Follow the instructions in Adding Bias Binding to Bag, Steps 1–3, to finish the pouch.

Emilia Quilted Bag

Finished size: 17" wide × 17" high (without the handles)

The Emilia Quilted Bag is a stunning bag with beautiful curves. It has a magnetic snap closure and simple curved piecing. Give it a try!

MATERIALS

note

You can choose to make the Emilia Quilted Bag with patchwork on just one side by using plain fabric on the back. Instructions assume patchwork on both the front and back.

18″ × 20″ (fat quarter) of 12 different fabrics for patchwork **OR** 1 yard of 44″-wide linen/cotton, home decor, or quilting-weight cotton fabric for one-fabric exterior

½ yard of solid color for handles

1 yard of 44″-wide quilting-weight cotton for lining

2 yards of 20″-wide heavy-weight fusible interfacing

18 mm magnetic snap

6″ all-purpose zipper for lining pocket

note

• *A ⅜″ seam allowance is included for the patchwork.*

• *A ⅜″ seam allowance is included on the patterns.*

• *Backstitch at the beginning and end of each seam.*

Patchwork

CUTTING

• Using the Emilia Quilted Bag patterns 1–12 (pullout page P3), cut the pieces and transfer all points and references to the fabric.

1. Place piece 12 and piece 11 with right sides together and pin in place. Sew and clip the curved seam (see Trimming and Clipping the Seam, page 7). Press the seam toward piece 11.

2. Repeat Step 1 to attach piece 10.

3. Follow Step 1 to attach piece 9.

4. Sew together pieces 1–8 in the same manner. Press the seams toward one side. FIGURE A

5. Sew the 2 units together. Press the seam toward the top of the bag. FIGURE B

6. Repeat Steps 1–5 for the other side of the bag.

Bag Construction

Using the Emilia Quilted Bag Front and Back, Emilia Quilted Bag Handle, and Zipper Pocket patterns (pullout pages P2–P4), cut out the following pieces and transfer all points and references to the fabric.

A

CUTTING

Exterior

• Cut 4 Handles (2 and 2 reversed).

Lining

• Cut 1 Front.

• Cut 1 Back.

• Cut 2 Zipper Pockets.

Interfacing

• Cut 1 Front.

• Cut 1 Back.

B

Exterior and Handles

1. Pin a handle onto the front exterior with right sides together. Match point A and stitch in place. **FIGURE C**

2. Clip the curved seam. **FIGURE D**

3. Repeat Steps 1 and 2 for adding the other handle to the front and for adding handles to the back. **FIGURE E**

4. Fuse the interfacing onto the wrong side of exterior patchwork. Quilt by hand or machine.

5. Lay the front exterior piece wrong side up. Pin and stitch along a dart line, backstitching at beginning and end. Repeat for the remaining darts in the front and back exterior pieces. **FIGURE F**

6. Press darts to the outside of the bag on the front and to the bottom of the bag on the back.

7. Pin the front and back exterior pieces with right sides together. Stitch around, making a U shape and backstitching at both ends. **FIGURE G**

8. Clip the curved seams.

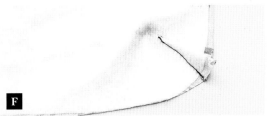

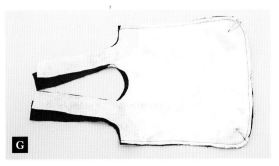

Lining

1. Attach the lining zipper pocket (see Zipper Pocket, page 10).

2. Apply the magnetic snap (see Applying a Magnetic Snap, page 6). **FIGURE A**

3. Repeat Exterior and Handles, Steps 5–8 (page 73), to assemble the lining. Leave a 5″ opening at the bottom for turning. **FIGURE B**

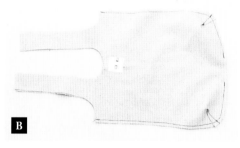

4. Press the exterior and lining seams open. Turn the exterior right side out. Insert the exterior inside the lining with right sides together. **FIGURE C**

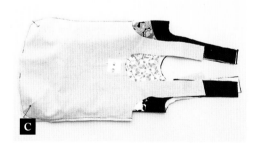

5. Pin the exterior and lining pieces together at the curved seam from the top of a handle to the top of the other handle. Sew, leaving the top 2″ of the handles unsewn. Then pin each of the remaining curves and sew in the same manner. Leave the top of the handles unstitched. **FIGURE D**

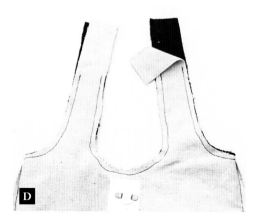

6. Clip the inside corner seam allowances and trim the seams. **FIGURE E**

7. Turn the bag right side out through the bottom opening. Sew the opening closed.

8. Tuck the lining into the exterior. Place the exterior handles with right sides together. Pin and sew together along the short edges. Press. Repeat this process for the lining. **FIGURE F**

9. Tuck in the raw edges of the seam allowances on both sides of the handles and press. **FIGURE G**

10. With wrong sides together, pin or baste the lining and exterior together at the handle opening. Topstitch ⅛″ from the seam around the armhole of the bag. Topstitch the other armhole and the main opening of the bag. **FIGURE H**

E

F

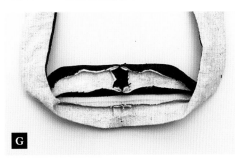

G

H

Mackenzie Messenger Bag

Finished size: 16" wide × 8½" high × 4½" deep

The Mackenzie Messenger Bag has a flap along with a zipper. Designed to fit perfectly on your shoulders, this bag was made with comfort in mind. Inside, the bag includes pockets on both sides—zipped or elastic, your choice—to allow for secure storage of important items such as keys and phones.

MATERIALS

Exterior

18″ × 20″ (fat quarter) of approximately 17 different fabrics for patchwork **OR** 1 yard of 44″-wide linen/cotton, home decor, or quilting weight-cotton fabric for one-fabric exterior

1 yard of 44″-wide quilting-weight cotton for lining

¼ yard of 44″ wide linen/cotton, home decor, or quilting-weight cotton fabric for buckle straps

1⅜ yards of 20″-wide lightweight fusible interfacing

18″ all-purpose zipper for zipper closure

6″ all-purpose zipper for lining pocket

2 D-rings, 1¼″

2 swivel lobster clasps with 1½″ D-ring ends

1¼″-wide slider strap adjuster

2 roller buckles with heel bar, 1¼″-wide (30 mm) inner diameter

Set of 8 metal eyelets, 6 mm (inside diameter ¼″, outside diameter ⁷⁄₁₆″)

Eyelet setter tools to fit 6 mm eyelets

2 yards of 1¼″-wide webbing for strap

8″ of 1″-wide hook-and-loop tape (non-fusible) for front pockets and flap

note
• *A ¼″ seam allowance is included for the patchwork.*

• *A ⅜″ seam allowance is included on the patterns.*

• *Backstitch at the beginning and end of each seam.*

Patchwork

CUTTING

Variety of fabrics

• Cut 228 pieces using the Mackenzie Messenger Bag Template A pattern or 117 pieces using Mackenzie Messenger Bag Template B pattern (pullout page P3).

----

1. For Template A, lay out the pieces in 12 rows of 19 pieces. For Template B, lay out the pieces in 9 rows of 13 pieces.

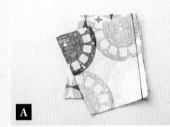

2. Place 2 of the pieces with right sides together, as shown. Pin and sew together, backstitching at both ends. Press.
FIGURES A & B

3. Continue the process from Step 2 to sew the pieces into rows. Press.
FIGURE C

4. Assemble the rows. Press.

Bag Construction

Using the Mackenzie Messenger Bag Front and Back, Mackenzie Messenger Bag Flap, Mackenzie Messenger Bag Gusset, Mackenzie Messenger Bag Front Pocket, and Zipper Pocket patterns (pullout pages P2 and P3), cut out the following pieces and transfer all points and references to the fabric.

CUTTING

Exterior

- Cut 1 Front (from patchwork or exterior fabric).

- Cut 1 Back (from patchwork or exterior fabric).

- Cut 2 Gusset pieces (from patchwork or exterior fabric).

- Cut 1 Flap piece (from patchwork or exterior fabric).

- Cut 2 Front Pocket pieces (from patchwork or exterior fabric).

- Cut 2 pieces 2″ × 14½″ for zipper panel (from leftover patchwork fabric).

- Cut 2 pieces 2″ × 3″ for zipper ends (from leftover patchwork fabric).

- Cut 2 pieces 4½″ × 2½″ for handle loops.

Exterior for straps

- Cut 2 pieces 5″ × 14″ for buckle strap.

- Cut 2 pieces 5″ × 2″ for buckle holder.

- Cut 2 pieces 1¼″ × 3¼″ for buckle holder loop.

Lining

- Cut 1 Front.

- Cut 1 Back.

- Cut 2 Gusset pieces.

- Cut 1 Flap piece.

- Cut 2 pieces 2″ × 14½″ for zipper panel.

- Cut 2 Front Pocket pieces.

- Cut 2 Zipper Pocket pieces.

Interfacing

- Cut 1 Front.

- Cut 1 Back.

- Cut 2 Gusset pieces.

- Cut 1 Flap piece.

Front Pockets

1. Cut 4 pieces of hook-and-loop tape, 1½″ each, and separate the tape. Place one side of the tape onto the front pocket exterior pieces and the front pocket lining pieces as indicated on the pattern. Pin and stitch around the hook-and-loop tape in a rectangle, backstitching at both ends. I recommend stitching all around the pocket exterior pieces ¼″ from the edge to prevent raveling.
FIGURE A

2. Pin and stitch the corner darts on the wrong side of the pocket exterior pieces as indicated on the pattern, backstitching at both ends. Repeat this process for the darts on the pocket lining pieces. On the pocket exterior pieces, press the darts toward the outside of the pocket; on the lining pieces, press the darts toward the center.
FIGURE B

3. Place the pocket exterior piece into the pocket lining piece with right sides together. Pin the pieces together, matching them at the sides and the dart seams. Stitch around the whole pocket, leaving a 2½″ opening at the bottom for turning.
FIGURE C

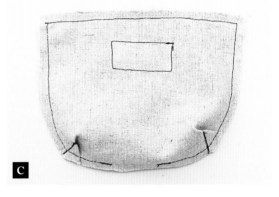

4. Turn the pocket right side out. Press and topstitch the top of the pocket ⅛″ from the edge. Repeat Steps 3 and 4 for the second pocket.
FIGURE D

5. Fuse the interfacing to the wrong side of the front, back, gusset, and flap exterior pieces.

6. Quilt the patchwork by hand or machine.

7. Place the other side of 2 hook-and-loop tape pieces onto the front exterior piece as indicated on the pattern. Pin and stitch around the hook-and-loop tape in a rectangle, backstitching at both ends. **FIGURE E**

8. Pin the front pockets onto the front exterior piece as indicated on the pattern. The hook-and-loop tapes on the bag exterior should match up with the tape on the inside of the pockets. Topstitch ⅛″ from the edge around the sides and bottom of the pockets. **FIGURE F**

Bag Construction

1. Match gusset exterior pieces with right sides together. Pin and stitch the center seam. Open and press. Topstitch on each side ⅛″ from the seam for reinforcement. **FIGURE G**

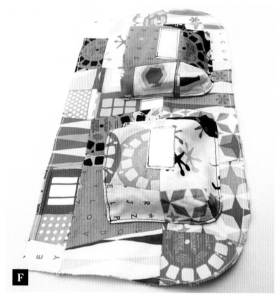

2. Pin the front exterior piece to the gusset piece, right sides together. Clip the gusset seam at the corners only as necessary to help ease the process around the curve of the front piece. Stitch all around the gusset and front pieces. Attach the back exterior piece to the other side of the gusset piece in a similar manner. **FIGURE H**

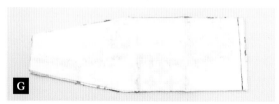

3. Clip and trim the curved seams. **FIGURE I**

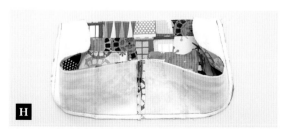

Flap and Buckles

1. Sew the buckle holders and the buckle holder loops (see Strap A, page 14). **FIGURE A**

2. Sew the buckle straps (see Strap B, page 14). **FIGURE B**

3. Install 3 eyelets 1¼″ apart into the finished end of each buckle strap and 1 eyelet into the middle of each buckle holder (see Installing an Eyelet, page 13). **FIGURE C**

4. Insert the buckle holder piece through the buckle bar side. Fold the buckle holder in half and stitch the end, backstitching at both ends. **FIGURE D**

5. Fold the buckle holder loop piece in half. Stitch the end of the buckle holder loop piece ⅜″ from the edge. Repeat Steps 4 and 5 for the second buckle holder piece. **FIGURE E**

6. Turn the buckle holder loop right side out. **FIGURE F**

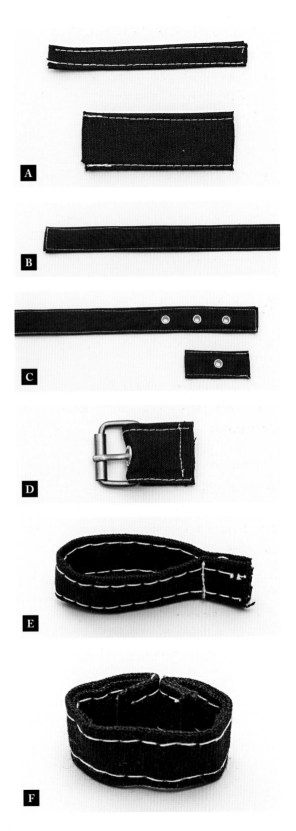

7. Insert the buckle holder into the buckle holder loop. Repeat Steps 6 and 7 for the second buckle holder loop. **FIGURE G**

8. Place the buckle holder onto the flap as indicated on the pattern. Baste the buckle holder ¼″ from the bottom of the flap. Attach the other buckle holder in the same manner. **FIGURE H**

9. Place the last 2 pieces of hook-and-loop tape onto the flap lining piece as indicated on the pattern. Pin and stitch around the hook-and-loop tape in a rectangular shape, backstitching at both ends.

10. Place the flap lining onto the flap exterior with right sides together. Pin and stitch 3 sides, leaving the top open and backstitching at both ends. **FIGURE I**

11. Turn the flap right side out. Press and topstitch ¼″ from the edge along 3 sides. **FIGURE J**

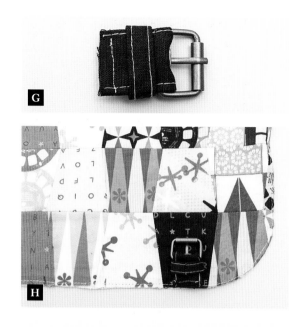

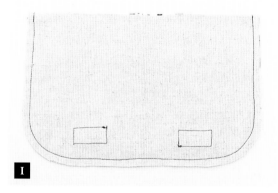

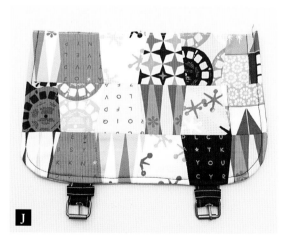

12. Place a buckle strap into one buckle. **FIGURE K**

13. Pin the buckle strap onto the flap. Stitch the strap on both sides ⅛″ from the edge, stopping 1½″ from the bottom of the flap. Trim the strap ½″ above the top edge of the flap. Repeat Steps 12 and 13 for the second buckle strap. **FIGURE L**

14. Turn the bag exterior right side out. Position the flap on the back piece of the bag exterior with exterior right sides together, aligning the raw edges. Baste together along the top edge. **FIGURE M**

15. Make the loops for the shoulder strap (see Strap A, page 14). **FIGURE N**

16. Insert one end of the loop through the D-ring and fold the loop in half. Baste close to the end. Repeat this process for the other loop piece.

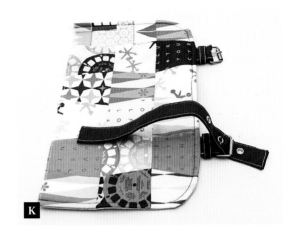

K

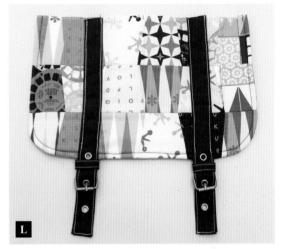

L

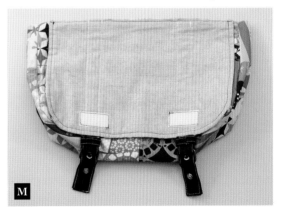

M

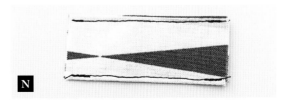

N

17. Center the raw end of the loop on the gusset exterior with right sides together. Pin and baste in place. Attach the other loop to the other side of the gusset in the same manner. **FIGURE O**

18. Make the lining zipper pocket (see Zipper Pocket, page 10).

19. Repeat Bag Construction, Steps 1–3 (page 80), with the lining pieces, leaving 5″ unstitched on one gusset seam along the bottom for turning the bag right side out.

Zipper

1. Fold all 4 sides of the zipper end pieces ⅜″ to the wrong side and press. Fold the piece in half widthwise, wrong sides together, and press to make a crease.

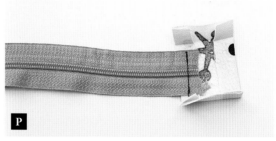

2. Unfold one side of the zipper end piece. Place the zipper onto the folded end of the zipper end piece and baste together. **FIGURE P**

3. Fold the zipper end piece again so that the end of the zipper is enclosed. Topstitch ⅛″ from the edges folded over the zipper. Attach the other side of the zipper end piece in the same manner. **FIGURE Q**

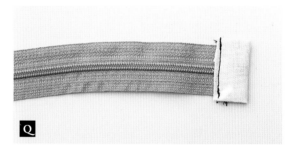

4. Fold each short end of the exterior zipper panels ⅜″ to the wrong side and press. Repeat this step for the lining zipper panel. **FIGURE R**

5. Install the zipper (see Scarlett Clutches, Install the Zipper, Steps 5–8, page 30) using the zipper panel exterior and zipper panel lining pieces.

6. Topstitch through all the layers ⅛″ from the edge of the zipper panels, next to the zipper. Baste the side edges of the zipper panel exterior and lining together ⅛″ from the other 3 edges. **FIGURE S**

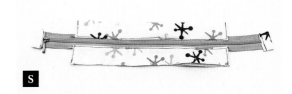

7. Open the zipper. Pin and baste the long edge of one zipper panel to the bag lining, with the lining side of zipper panel facing the right side of bag lining. Baste in place. Repeat this step to baste the other zipper panel to the other side of the bag lining. **FIGURE T**

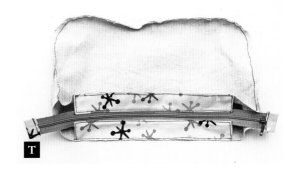

Assemble the Bag

1. Open the zipper. Press the exterior and lining seams open. Tuck the exterior into the lining with right sides together, sandwiching the flap and the zipper panels between them. **FIGURE U**

2. Pin and sew the top opening of the exterior and lining pieces, backstitching on both ends. **FIGURE V**

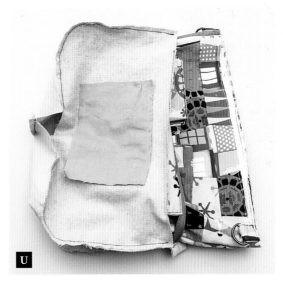

3. Trim the seams. Turn the bag right side out through the opening in the lining. Stitch the opening closed.

4. Tuck the lining into the exterior. Press the top opening of the bag. Topstitch around the opening ⅛″ from the edge.

5. Cut a piece of webbing 60″ long. Make the shoulder strap (see Connecting an Adjustable Buckle, page 7) and attach it to the bag.

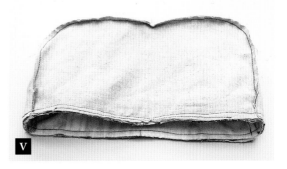

Hexagon Backpack

Finished size: 12½" wide × 15¼" high × 4" deep

You can take this backpack anywhere, anytime! The hexagon patchwork is a real eye-catcher! Although the patchwork may look complicated at first, it will be easy once you get the hang of it. It can even become quite addicting! Since the bag is large, it can be a comfortable school bag or even a diaper bag. So convenient in many ways!

MATERIALS

18″ × 20″ (fat quarter) each of approximately 17 different fabrics for patchwork **OR** 1¼ yards of 44″-wide linen/cotton, home decor, or quilting-weight cotton fabric for one-fabric exterior

10″ × 11″ of soft leather for bottom gusset piece (optional)

1¼ yards of 44″-wide quilting-weight cotton for lining

2 yards of 20″-wide lightweight fusible interfacing

24″ all-purpose zipper

10″ all-purpose zipper for front pocket

6″ all-purpose zipper for lining pocket

½ yard of ⅜″-wide elastic for lining elastic pocket

3½ yards of ½″ double-fold bias tape for lining

2 plastic strap adjusters (ladderlock buckles) 1¼″ (30 mm) wide

1½ yards of 1¼″-wide webbing

2 webbing tips

> **note**
> • *A ¼″ seam allowance is included for the patchwork.*
> • *A ⅜″ seam allowance is included on the patterns.*
> • *Backstitch at the beginning and end of each seam.*

Patchwork

CUTTING

Variety of fabrics

• Cut 144 pieces using the Hexagon Backpack Hexagon A pattern or 110 pieces using the Hexagon Backpack Hexagon B pattern (pullout page P4).

1. For Hexagon A, lay out the pieces in 12 rows of 12 hexagons. For Hexagon B, lay out the pieces in 10 rows of 11 hexagons.

2. Place 2 hexagon pieces with right sides together. Stitch together along one straight edge, starting and ending ¼″ from the end of the seam at both ends. Backstitch on both ends. **FIGURE A**

A

3. Continue the process from Step 2 to sew the pieces into rows. **FIGURES B & C**

4. Sew the rows together, stitching in a Y shape along the seams and leaving ¼″ unsewn at each end. **FIGURES D & E**

5. Press the seams in the first row toward one side. Open the corner seams, as shown. Repeat this process for the seams in the remaining rows. **FIGURE F**

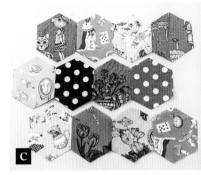

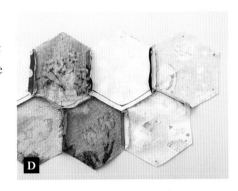

Backpack Construction

Using the Hexagon Backpack Front and Back, Hexagon Backpack Front Zipper Pocket (Top) and (Bottom), Hexagon Backpack Back Strap Holder, and Zipper Pocket patterns (pullout pages P2 and P4), cut out the following pieces and transfer all points and references to the fabric.

Exterior

• Cut 1 Front (from patchwork or exterior fabric).

• Cut 1 Back (from patchwork or exterior fabric).

• Cut 2 pieces 2½″ × 23¾″ for zipper panel (from patchwork or exterior fabric).

• Cut 2 pieces 4¾″ × 14¼″ for gusset (from patchwork or exterior fabric) or

• Cut 2 pieces of leather 4¾″ × 9½″ and 2 pieces 4¾″ × 5½″ (from patchwork or exterior fabric) and sew them together to make 2 pieces 4¾″ × 14¼″ (optional).

• Cut 1 Front Pocket (Top).

• Cut 1 Front Pocket (Bottom).

• Cut 2 pieces 2½″ × 1½″ for front pocket zipper ends.

• Cut 2 pieces 8″ × 16″ for straps.

• Cut 8 Back Strap Holders.

• Cut 2 pieces of webbing 14″ for back straps.

• Cut 2 pieces of webbing 5″ for ladderlock loops.

• Cut 1 piece of webbing 11″ for handle.

Lining

• Cut 1 Front.

• Cut 1 Back.

• Cut 2 pieces 2½″ × 23¾″ for zipper panel.

• Cut 2 pieces 4¾″ × 14¼″ for gusset.

• Cut 1 Front Pocket (Top).

• Cut 1 Front Pocket (Bottom).

• Cut 2 Zipper Pocket pieces.

• Cut 1 Elastic Pocket (see Elastic Pocket, page 9).

Bias binding

• Cut 2 strips 55″.

• Cut 2 strips 5″.

Interfacing

• Cut 1 Front.

• Cut 1 Back.

• Cut 2 pieces 2½″ × 23¾″ for zipper panel.

• Cut 2 pieces 4¾″ × 14¼″ for gusset.

• Cut 2 pieces 8″ × 16″ for straps.

Front Pocket

1. Place the front pocket zipper ends onto the ends of the front pocket zipper with right sides together. If your zipper is longer than 10″, measure from just before the zipper pull to 10″ and mark the zipper tape. Place the zipper end piece on the closed end of the zipper so that the edge of the fabric is ¼″ past the mark. Pin and stitch the zipper ends using a ¼″ seam. **FIGURE A**

2. Turn the zipper ends right side out and press the seam. Topstitch on the zipper ends, ⅛″ from the seam. Trim the zipper end pieces so they are the same width as the zipper tape. **FIGURE B**

3. Baste the front pocket bottom exterior and front pocket bottom lining together with wrong sides together. Baste together the front pocket top exterior and lining in the same manner. Place the front pocket zipper onto the front pocket bottom with right sides together. Pin and stitch close to the zipper coil, backstitching at both ends. **FIGURE C**

4. Flip the zipper toward the up side, and press the seam toward the bottom piece. Topstitch on the front pocket bottom ⅛″ from the seam. **FIGURE D**

5. Place the front pocket top piece onto the bottom piece with right sides together. The zipper will now be between the top and bottom pieces. Sew the front pocket top and zipper together close to the zipper coils, backstitching at both ends. **FIGURE E**

6. Flip the front pocket top piece up and press the seam toward the top piece. **FIGURE F**

A

B

C

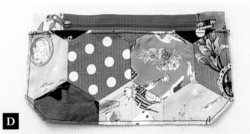

D

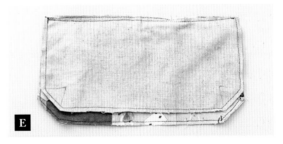

E

F

7. Fold the front pocket top piece down on the first folding line as indicated on the pattern. Fold the front pocket top piece up on the second folding line as indicated on the pattern. Topstitch on the folded front pocket top 1″ from the second folding line. **FIGURE G**

8. Pin and sew the 4 darts in the front pocket top and bottom, backstitching at both ends. **FIGURE H**

9. Overlock or zigzag the raw edges all around, if you wish. Flip the assembled pocket piece with the wrong side up and fold the seam in ⅜″ with wrong sides together. **FIGURE I**

10. Fuse interfacing to the wrong side of exterior pieces: front and back, gussets, fabric straps, and zipper panels. Quilt by hand or machine.

11. Place the front pocket onto the bag front piece as indicated on the pattern. Pin in place and topstitch around the pocket sides ⅛″ from the folded edges. **FIGURE J**

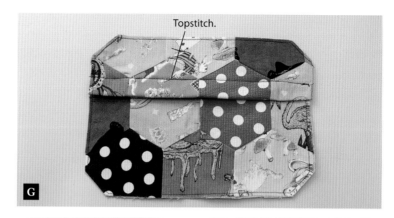

Topstitch.

G

H

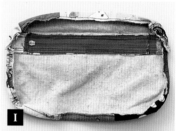

I

J

Back Straps

1. Fold and press a ½″ seam on one short end of the back strap. Then, fold the strap in half lengthwise with wrong sides together. Open the strap and fold each side in toward the center and press. **FIGURE A**

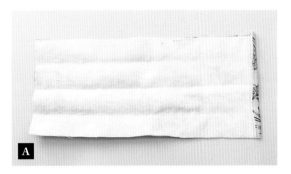

2. Insert one end of the webbing loop through the ladderlock buckle and fold the loop in half. Pin and baste the raw ends of the loop together to keep the buckle from slipping out. **FIGURE B**

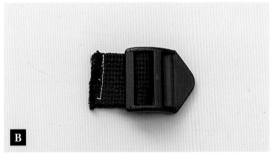

3. Place the buckle loop onto the folded end of the strap as shown and baste in place. Fold the sides of the strap toward the center crease. Fold along the center crease and press again. **FIGURE C**

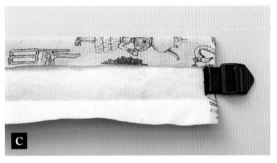

4. Pin and topstitch the strap ⅛″ from the edge around 3 edges, leaving the short, unfolded edge open. Repeat Steps 1–4 for the second strap. **FIGURE D**

5. Place 2 back strap holders with right sides together. Pin and sew the strap holder along the short sides, backstitching at both ends. Leave the bottom unstitched. Trim the corner seam. Repeat this process with the other 6 back strap holder pieces. **FIGURE E**

6. Turn the back strap holders right sides out and press. Place the webbing back strap onto the strap holder as indicated on the pattern and baste. **FIGURE F**

7. Place another assembled back strap holder centered onto the first strap holder, aligning the raw edges. Pin and topstitch the holder ⅛″ from the edge. **FIGURE G**

8. Thread the webbing back strap up behind the buckle and out again through the 2 bars. Thread it over the rung and back down under the bottom tongue of the buckle. Pull down on the strap to tighten it. Lift the tongue of the buckle to loosen it. Repeat Steps 6–8 for the second strap. Buckle a webbing tip onto the raw end of each strap. **FIGURE H**

9. Place the assembled back straps onto the back piece as indicated on the pattern. Pin at the top of each strap and where the strap holders attach at the sides of the bag. Baste to hold in place. **FIGURE I**

Zipper

1. Install the zipper (see Scarlett Clutches, Install the Zipper, Steps 5–8, page 30) using the exterior and lining zipper panel pieces. **FIGURE A**

2. Assemble the zipper panel and gusset (see Glenda Boston Bag, Bag Zipper Panels and Gusset Panel, Step 2–7, page 67). **FIGURE B**

Assemble the Bag

1. Insert a zipper pocket in the front lining piece (see Zipper Pocket, page 10).

2. Insert an elastic pocket in the back lining piece (see Elastic Pocket, page 9).

3. Pin and baste the front exterior and front lining pieces, wrong sides together. Pin the front piece to the assembled gusset piece with exterior right sides together. Pin the centers and zipper ends first, and then pin the rest of the seam. Sew the front and gusset together, backstitching on both ends. Unzip the zipper. Attach the back exterior and back lining in the same manner. **FIGURES C & D**

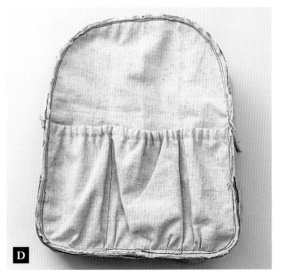

Bias Binding

Add the bias tape all the way around the 2 long gusset/zipper panel seams (see Chloe Bag, Bag Body, Steps 6–8, page 52). Turn the bag right side out through the zipper.

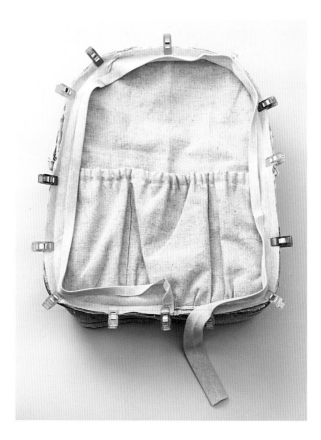

Eva Big Bag

Finished size: 24" wide × 15½" high (without the strap) × 6" deep

This big shoulder bag is a simple, beginner-friendly project made using patchwork blocks. It's large enough to store all of your most important belongings and is perfect in both style and comfort.

MATERIALS

9–11 different fat quarters (18″ × 20″) for exterior patchwork **OR** 2 yards 44″-wide linen/cotton, home decor, or quilting-weight cotton fabric for one-fabric exterior

2 yards of 44″-wide quilting-weight cotton for lining

3 yards of 20″-wide lightweight fusible interfacing

6″ all-purpose zipper for lining pocket

18 mm magnetic snap

note
- *A ¼″ seam allowance is included for the patchwork.*
- *A ⅜″ seam allowance is included on the patterns.*
- *Backstitch at the beginning and end of each seam.*

Patchwork

CUTTING

Fat quarters

- Cut 104 squares 5″ × 5″.

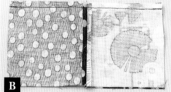

1. Place 2 squares with right sides together. Pin and stitch along one side. Press. Repeat this step with 2 more squares. **FIGURE A**

2. Place the units made in Step 1 with right sides together. Pin and stitch to make a four-patch unit. Press. **FIGURES B & C**

3. Make another four-patch unit following Steps 1 and 2.

4. Place the four-patch units with right sides together. Pin all sides and stitch around the square ¼″ from the edges. Draw a diagonal line from corner to corner in each direction. **FIGURE D**

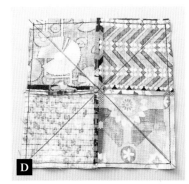

D

5. Using a rotary cutter, cut on the drawn lines. **FIGURE E**

6. Open these quarter-square triangle blocks and press. Trim each block to 6″ × 6″. **FIGURE F**

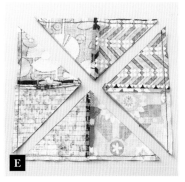

E

TIP ‖ When you trim, make sure the diagonal seams come through the exact corner of the block by matching the 45° line on your cutting ruler with the diagonal seamlines.

note
Eight squares will yield four quarter-square triangle blocks.

F

7. Repeat Steps 1–6 to make 52 quarter-square triangle blocks.

8. Arrange the blocks as shown.

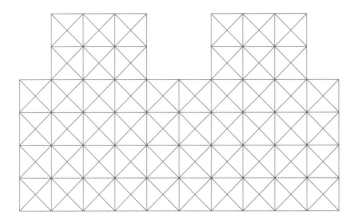

9. Sew the blocks into rows. Then sew the rows together. Press.

Bag Construction

Using the Eva Big Bag Front and Back and Zipper Pocket patterns (pullout pages P2 and P4), cut out the following pieces and transfer all points and references to the fabric.

CUTTING

Exterior

• Cut 1 Front (from patchwork or exterior fabric).

• Cut 1 Back (from patchwork or exterior fabric).

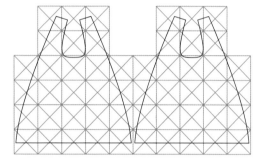

Lining

• Cut 1 Front.

• Cut 1 Back.

• Cut 2 Zipper Pockets.

• Cut 2 pieces 12″ × 7″ for lining pocket.

Interfacing

note

You will need to cut your interfacing in half crosswise and join it along the longer edges to create a piece wide enough for this pattern. Overlap the edges by ¼″, pin, and stitch the pieces together.

• Cut 1 Front.

• Cut 1 Back.

Exterior and Lining

1. Fuse interfacing on the wrong side of the front and back exterior, following the manufacturer's instructions.

2. Quilt by hand or machine.

3. Place the front and back pieces with right sides together, pin both sides, and stitch. Pin the bottom and stitch together. **FIGURE A**

4. Match the side and bottom seams with right sides together. Pin in place and stitch. Repeat this process for the other side. **FIGURE B**

5. Attach the magnetic snap to the front and back lining pieces (see Applying a Magnetic Snap, page 6).

6. Sew the lining pocket and the zipper pocket (see Standard Pocket, page 8 and Zipper Pocket, page 10). **FIGURE C**

7. Sew the lining pieces together following Steps 3 and 4 above. Leave a 6″ opening for turning. **FIGURE D**

8. Press the exterior and lining seams open. Turn the exterior right side out. Insert the exterior inside the lining with right sides together. **FIGURE E**

9. Pin the exterior and lining pieces together at the curved seam from the top of one handle to the top of the other handle. Sew, leaving the top 2˝ of the handles unsewn. Then pin the remaining curve and sew in the same manner. Leave the top of the handles unstitched. **FIGURE F**

10. Clip the inside seam allowances (see Clipping and Trimming the Seam, page 7). **FIGURE G**

11. Turn the bag right side out through the opening in the lining. Press; then stitch the lining opening closed.

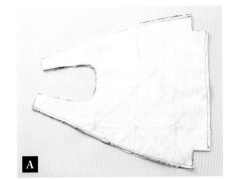

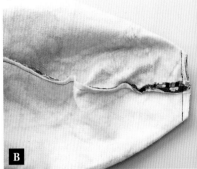

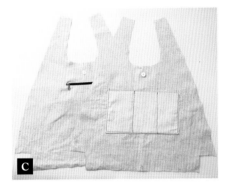

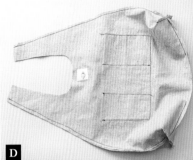

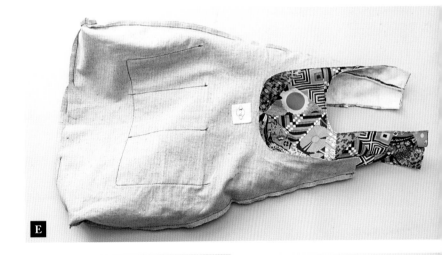

Handle

1. Tuck the lining into the exterior. Place the exterior handles with right sides together. Pin and sew together along the short edges. Press. Repeat this process for the lining.

2. Turn in the raw edges of the seam allowances on both sides of the straps and press.

3. Pin or baste the lining to the strap, wrong sides together along the opening. Topstitch ⅛″ from the edge around each side of the armhole of the bag.

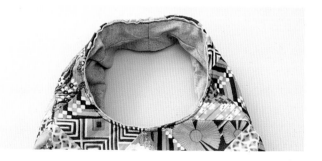

Delilah Cross Bag

Finished size: 9¼″ wide × 7¾″ high × 1″ deep

This delightful cross bag, with its easy-to-sew flap patchwork, is a great project for the beginning quilter. It is not too big and is perfectly designed for both style and simplicity.

MATERIALS

6–9 (or more) different fat eighths for flap exterior patchwork

⅜ yard of 44″-wide linen/cotton, home decor, or quilting-weight cotton fabric for exterior or exterior and one-fabric flap

⅝ yard of 44″-wide quilting-weight cotton for lining

1 yard of 20″-wide lightweight fusible interfacing

6″ all-purpose zipper for lining pocket

2½ yards of webbing (1″–1⅛″ wide) for strap

18 mm magnetic snap (optional)

3 swivel snap hooks, 1¼″

3 D-rings, 1¼″

1 slider strap adjuster, 1¼″

note

• *A ¼″ seam allowance is included for the patchwork.*

• *A ⅜″ seam allowance is included on the patterns.*

• *Backstitch at the beginning and end of each seam.*

Flap Patchwork

CUTTING

Fat eighths

• Cut a total of 9 squares 3½″ × 3½″.

• Cut 9 strips 1″ × 8″.

1. Fold a square in half with wrong sides together and press. Using a rotary cutter, cut in half along the crease. **FIGURE A**

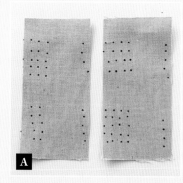

2. Place one of the 1″ × 8″ strips onto one long edge of a half square with right sides together. Pin and stitch together. Flip the strip away from the half square and press. **FIGURE B**

3. Attach the other half square to the remaining side of the strip, flip outward, and press. Trim the strip even with the square. **FIGURE C**

4. Cut the unit in half the opposite way. **FIGURE D**

5. Attach the remaining piece of the strip in the same manner as Steps 2 and 3 and press. Repeat Steps 1–5 for a total of 9 blocks. **FIGURE E**

6. Arrange the blocks into 3 rows of 3 blocks each. **FIGURE F**

7. Sew the blocks into rows and then sew the rows together. Press. **FIGURE G**

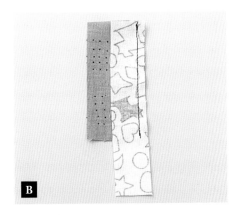

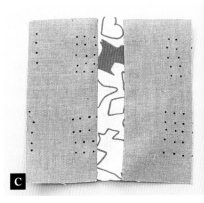

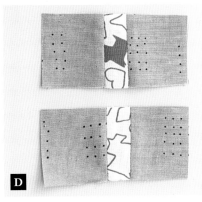

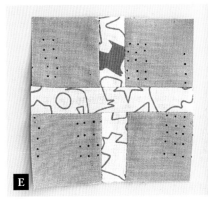

Bag Construction

Using the Delilah Cross Bag Front and Back and Delilah Cross Bag Flap patterns (pullout page P4), cut out the following pieces and transfer all points and references to the fabric.

- -

CUTTING

Exterior

- Cut 1 Flap (from patch-work or exterior fabric).
- Cut 1 Front.
- Cut 1 Back.
- Cut 2 pieces 1¾″ × 12⅝″ for gusset.
- Cut 2 pieces 2¼″ × 4¼″ for strap loops.

Lining

- Cut 1 Flap.
- Cut 1 Front.
- Cut 1 Back.
- Cut 2 pieces 1¾″ × 12⅝″ for gusset.
- Cut 2 Zipper Pocket pieces.

Interfacing

- Cut 1 Front.
- Cut 1 Back.
- Cut 1 Flap.
- Cut 2 pieces 1¾″ × 12⅝″ for gusset.

- -

Flap

1. Fuse the interfacing on the wrong side of the front and back exterior pieces, the gusset pieces, and the flap, following the manufacturer's instructions.

2. Quilt the flap by hand or machine.

3. Attach one part of the magnetic snap (optional) to the right side of the flap lining piece and the other part of the snap to the front exterior piece (see Applying a Magnetic Snap, page 6).

4. Place the flap exterior and flap lining with right sides together. Pin and sew along the 2 side edges and the bottom, backstitching on both ends. Leave the top opening unstitched. Clip the round seams (see Clipping and Trimming the Seam, page 7). **FIGURE A**

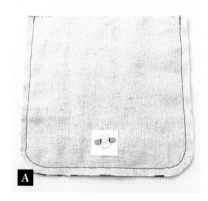

A

5. Turn the flap right side out. Press and topstitch ¼″ from the edge. **FIGURE B**

6. Cut a piece of webbing 9½″. Center the webbing strap vertically onto the assembled flap. Stitch the webbing strap to the flap on both sides for 6″ down from the top. **FIGURE C**

7. Insert the loose end of the webbing into a swivel snap hook. Fold ½″ from the end of the strap. Fold the strap over the swivel snap hook. Adjust it so that the hook ends just below the bottom of the flap and pin in place. Sew the strap together in a rectangle. **FIGURE D**

8. Cut a piece of webbing 2¾″. Insert one end of the webbing through a D-ring and fold the loop in half. Pin and baste the raw ends of the loop together to keep the D-ring from slipping out. **FIGURE E**

9. Place the folded webbing loop on the bottom of the front exterior piece, as shown, and pin. **FIGURE F**

B

C

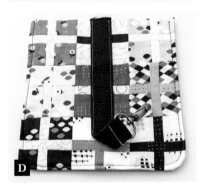

D

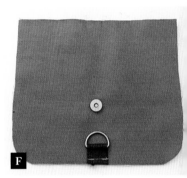

E

F

Exterior

1. Match the gusset exterior pieces with right sides together. Pin and stitch the center seam and press. Topstitch on each side ⅛″ from the seam for reinforcement. **FIGURE A**

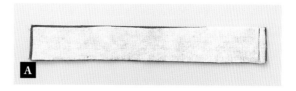

2. Pin the front piece to the gusset piece with right sides together. Clip the gusset seam only as necessary to help ease it around the curve of the front piece. Stitch all around the gusset and front pieces. Attach the back piece to the other side of the gusset piece in the same way. **FIGURE B**

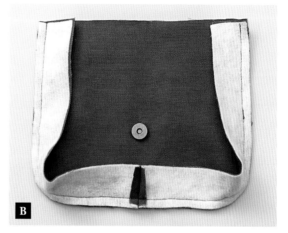

3. Clip and trim the seams (see Clipping and Trimming the Seam, page 7). **FIGURE C**

4. Turn the bag exterior right side out. Position the flap on the back piece of the bag exterior with exterior right sides together, aligning the raw edges. Pin and then baste the 2 pieces together. **FIGURE D**

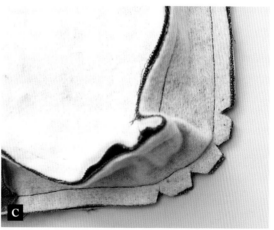

5. Make the strap loops (see Strap A, page 14).

6. Insert one end of the loop through the D-ring and fold the loop in half. Baste close to the end. Repeat this process for the other loop piece.

7. Center the raw end of the loop on the gusset exterior, right sides together. Pin and baste in place. Construct the other loop and attach it to the other side of the gusset in the same manner. **FIGURE E**

Lining

1. Repeat Exterior, Steps 1–3, with the lining pieces, leaving 5″ unstitched along one gusset seam for turning. **FIGURE F**

2. Press the exterior and lining seams open. Insert the exterior into the lining, right sides together. The flap and ring loops should all be sandwiched between the lining and exterior. **FIGURE G**

3. Pin the exterior and lining together around the opening of the bag. Stitch around the opening of the bag. **FIGURE H**

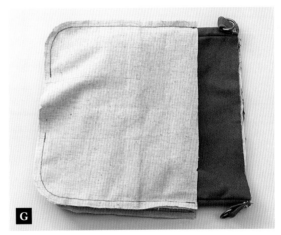

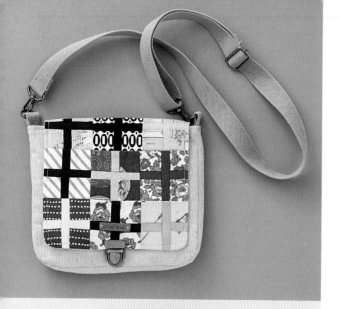

4. Turn the bag right side out through the hole in the lining. Sew the opening in the lining closed. Tuck the lining into the exterior. Press the top opening of the bag. Topstitch around the opening ¼″ from the edge.

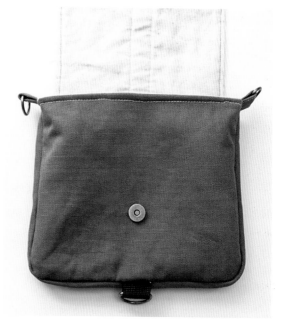

5. Cut a piece of webbing 60″ long. Make an adjustable strap (see Connecting an Adjustable Buckle, page 7) and attach it to the D-rings at the sides of the bag.

110

Perfect Patchwork Bags

About the Authors

Sue Kim

Sue Kim shares her patterns and creativity on her popular website, ithinksew.com. She started sewing when she was ten years old and has always had a passion for crafts. She earned a master's degree in ancient Asian theater. However, she kept sewing and designing as a hobby until, luckily, she was asked to be a sewing instructor at a Jo-Ann Fabric and Craft Store. That expanded into requests to teach in several quilt shops. The quilt shop owners also encouraged her to start her own pattern business.

Her first patterns were for small bags and clutches, and eventually she was asked to make a pattern book of bags and clutches. Many of the patterns Sue sells are downloadable PDF patterns.

Sue has completed several books of patterns and has become an independent pattern designer who is now writing for several publishers and pattern companies.

Her website can be found at ithinksew.com; her fabrics can also be viewed at spoonflower.com/profiles/ithinksew.

Veronica Yang

Most people would start off by introducing when they started sewing, but the thing is, Veronica can't remember! She's always had a passion for art in general, and sewing was just an activity she grew up with, as second nature. It may have helped to have a mother (Sue Kim) who was working in the field and who had a strong love for the art. Veronica often used her spare time to draw and design her own creations, from celebrity dresses to simple tops. Her sketchbook was always full of creations that she would dream of designing one day. And now, to see something of hers in a book is just amazing! She hopes to keep doing this with the same love and care she's seen her mother do for all her life.

111

About the Authors